D0427184

*Military Justice and
the Right to Counsel*

MILITARY JUSTICE AND
THE RIGHT TO COUNSEL

S. Sidney Ulmer

The University Press of Kentucky

LEXINGTON 1970

Library of Congress Catalog Card Number 74-94074
Standard Book Number 8131-1202-8

To Margaret

Contents

Acknowledgments

The author is indebted to David Fellman for his encouragement and to the Institute on American Freedoms for supporting the research on which this study is based.

Military Justice and
the Right to Counsel

Introduction

In social and political systems, two questions are always paramount: What behavior is to be controlled and what methods are to be employed? Citizens, philosophers, governments, and gods are continuously agreeing and disagreeing about adequate answers to these questions. Out of such disputes grow international treaties and alliances, schools of philosophy and political theory, constitutions for government, statutes, and court decisions. All provide answers that emphasize the relative importance of the two sides of the issue as well as the acceptable posture to be taken on each.

In Western democracies, suppression of undesirable behavior is often attempted through removal of the transgressor from the larger society. In turn, those responsible for the removal are subjected to due process and other restrictions in discharging their responsibilities. While control of behavior is an element in both cases, a distinction may be made between the actor who has a legally defined status in the sanctioning process and one who is to be sanctioned for behaving improperly.

It has never been thought that behavioral controls should be applied equally across all possible subcultures in a larger society. In the United States, at least three distinct subcultures can be identified: the criminal society, the military society, and the citizens' society—composed of those who do not fall in the first two categories. Each of these societies has had its own set of controls and a rationale which at some point in the development of the social and political system has been granted legitimacy. However, as ignorance diminishes and values change, political systems are subjected to tensions which usually lead to appropriate adjustments. A viable system is one that makes these adjustments at a relatively low tension level and without undue disruption. This is more likely to occur in regard to the needs of the more visible or citizens' society than in response to the demands of criminal or military subcultures. If this were not so, prison riots would be unnecessary. But the dramatic event is sometimes required in the citizens' society and is frequently effective as evidenced by the gun control law growing out of Robert Kennedy's assassination and Martin Luther King, Jr.'s murder.

In the military system the recent "*Pueblo* incident" has served to alert us to some of the disparities between our military and civilian systems and has provided fuel for the fires of change. The *Pueblo* was a 906-ton intelligence ship operating under the sponsorship of the United States Navy in waters off the coast of North Korea. The vessel carried secret electronic equipment that had the capacity to intercept radar signals and collect other types of intelligence data. It was under the command of Lloyd M. Bucher and was under orders not to penetrate the twelve-mile limit claimed by the North Koreans as their territorial waters. On January 23, 1968, North Korean patrol boats seized the *Pueblo,* with its eighty-three crewmembers, and escorted it into Wonsan Harbor, alleging that the ship had violated North Korean waters on a "spy mission."[1]

The military systems of all nations attempt to provide, in their contingency planning, for all probable events that may affect national security. This planning leads to "if—then" policy statements which prescribe the appropriate military response if the stated contingency occurs. Obviously, this is an attempt to control behavior under stated conditions. The concept is extended to individual servicemen through rules, regulations, and laws that describe

[1] *New York Times,* 24 January 1968, p. 1.

prohibited behavior and expected behavior under certain conditions. Thus an immediate question raised by the seizure of the *Pueblo* was: Did the commander and his crew behave properly during the capture?

Such a question is never academic, since improper behavior can lead to severe penalties. In 1807 when the Napoleonic War was at its peak, the fifty-two gun British flagship *Leopard* seized the United States frigate *Chesapeake* just outside territorial waters off the coast of Virginia. The *Chesapeake,* under the command of Commodore James Barron, did not surrender, however, until after three broadsides had killed three of Barron's men and wounded eighteen others.[2] Court-martialed, Barron was suspended from duty for five years on the ground that he neglected to clear his ship for action despite the probability of an engagement. It has long been a navy tradition not to surrender any ship without a fight. But the *Chesapeake* affair illustrates, additionally, that reasonable preparation to fight is necessary to avoid the charge of probable negligence.

An attack on the *Pueblo* was not anticipated. Consequently, she was armed only with two fifty-caliber machineguns and some side arms. To capture the ship, the North Koreans fired upon it and wounded eleven men including Bucher. One of the crewmen, Duane Hodges, was wounded while resisting the boarding party and subsequently died. In return the *Pueblo* did not fire its machineguns and the captain chose to save the crew, as he put it, rather than abide by naval regulations forbidding a skipper to surrender his ship to an enemy or a stranger as long as he has the power to resist.[3]

[2] Richard B. Morris, ed., *Encyclopedia of American History* (New York, 1953), pp. 136-37.

[3] *Louisville Courier-Journal,* 4 March 1969, p. A9. Although Bucher earlier used the term "surrender" to describe the transfer of the *Pueblo* to the North Koreans, he later took the position that transfer occurred as a consequence of seizure (*New York Times,* 12 March 1969, p. C18) and asserted vigorously that at time of seizure, the *Pueblo* lacked the power to resist (*New York Times,* 14 March 1969, p. C18). However, his attorney on the same day told the Court of Inquiry that any at-

3

Even more controversial behavior was to follow, an assessment of which requires a proper perspective. A military person is created during his initial training which emphasizes depersonalization, isolation, and reorganization. It becomes clear immediately to those who go through this basic training that the sloppy, the arrogant, and the independent are out of place in the service. The investment required on the part of the civilian inductee to this new life is difficult, but his alternatives are limited. He cannot strike, desert, quit his job, or mutiny. If uncooperative and brought to trial, he knows that he has no right to jury trial or bail and that, in general, he is part of a highly undemocratic organization. In short the expectations which hold for the military person are sufficiently different from those which apply to the civilian that a "remaking" of the person is necessary if the desired behavior is to result.

To enforce a reorientation of the person, the traditional Articles of War have always specified controls on the behavior of the serviceman and the penalties to be levied for violation of its provisions. In 1951 the Congress adopted the Uniform Code of Military Justice (UCMJ), which replaced the Articles of War, and set up a Court of Military Appeals as the supreme court of the military. The major controls on the behavior of the military person are now encompassed in the UCMJ (as amended), in the Manual of Courts Martial and service regulations that interpret the code, and in the Code of Conduct promulgated by executive order of the president in 1955.[4]

The Code of Conduct came into being as a result of the experiences of American prisoners of war during the Korean

---

tempt to man the fifty-caliber machineguns would have been suicidal (ibid.). This makes it very clear that the attempt was not ordered by Bucher, thereby providing the issue as to whether such an order should have been given.

[4] Executive Order 10631, *Code of Conduct for Members of the Armed Forces of the United States*, 17 August 1955. For a recent discussion of the *Code* and its implications, see Elizabeth R. Smith, Jr., "The Code of Conduct in Relation to International Law," *Military Law Review* 31 (Jan. 1966): 85-135.

Conflict. Its six provisions describe the behavior desired by our defense authorities under specified conditions and read as follows:

I

I am an American fighting man. I serve in the forces which guard my country and our way of life. I am prepared to give my life in their defense.

II

I will never surrender of my own free will. If in command, I will never surrender my men while they still have the means to resist.

III

If I am captured I will continue to resist by all means available. I will make every effort to escape and aid others to escape. I will accept neither parole nor special favors from the enemy.

IV

If I become a prisoner of war, I will keep faith with my fellow prisoners. I will give no information nor take part in any action which might be harmful to my comrades. If I am senior, I will take command. If not, I will obey the lawful orders of those appointed over me and will back them up in every way.

V

When questioned, should I become a prisoner of war, I am bound to give only name, rank, service number, and date of birth. I will evade answering further questions to the utmost of my ability. I will make no oral or written statements disloyal to my country and its allies or harmful to their cause.

VI

I will never forget that I am an American fighting man, responsible for my actions, and dedicated to the principles which made my country free. I will trust in my God and in the United States of America.

In promulgating the code, President Eisenhower said, "Every member of the Armed Forces of the United States is expected to measure up to the standards embodied in this

Code of Conduct while he is in combat or in captivity."[5] It was the intent that the member of the armed forces in combat or captivity have a clear understanding of the prevailing behavioral expectations under varying conditions. But what if these expectations are violated? What if this attempt at controlling the behavior of the serviceman by implanting certain inhibitions, in a given instance, fails? Such questions assumed significant proportions as a result of the behavior of Commander Bucher and his crew after capture.

The North Koreans were quick to charge that Bucher had confessed to violating North Korean waters, the confessions being made on radio, allegedly by Bucher on January 25.[6] A picture, apparently of Bucher writing his confession, was circulated several days later.[7] As for the radio broadcast, Bucher's wife said it was not her husband's voice, and a former shipmate, Alan P. Hemphill, declared, "It sounded like some semi-illiterate creep. I couldn't tell whose voice it was, but I'm quite sure it wasn't Bucher's."[8] Later other officers and crewmen were said to have confessed to spying.[9] But again the confessions were disbelieved. In July the House Armed Services Committee approved a bill to pay each member of the *Pueblo* crew sixty-five dollars a month in hostile-fire pay retroactive to January and to end the month after being freed by North Korea.[10] The controller general had ruled that such payment was illegal, since the ship was not operating in a designated hostile area when captured. In September, however, President Johnson signed the bill, thereby circumventing the controller general.[11] It appears that the government and the American people both rejected the confessions not

[5] *New York Times,* 18 August 1955, p. 1.

[6] Ibid., 25 January 1968, p. 1; Ibid., 26 January 1968, p. 10.

[7] Ibid., 27 January 1968, p. 7.

[8] Ibid., 26 January 1968, p. 10.

[9] Ibid., 3 February 1968, p. 5; Ibid., 5 February 1968, p. 14; Ibid., 13 February 1968, p. 12; Ibid., 5 March 1968, p. 1.

[10] Ibid., 12 July 1968, p. 11.

[11] Ibid., 24 September 1968, p. 36.

6

only because of a refusal to believe that the *Pueblo* in fact had violated North Korean waters but also because of a widespread belief that the admonishments to give "only name, rank, service number, and date of birth" and to "make no oral or written statements disloyal to my country" would, as a matter of course, be honored. Thus, upon the release of the commander and his crew in December 1968, Rear Admiral Edwin M. Rosenberg called Bucher "a hero among heroes" and said that the ship's crew "at all times acted in an extremely honorable fashion." He added that there would be a "routine court of inquiry."[12]

A court of inquiry is neither a court-martial nor a trial. It is a preliminary hearing designed to gather facts and to determine if any further action is necessary. Normally, such courts are fairly routine and undramatic. In this case, however, great public interest in the matter made a daily continuing drama of the court and the testimony being offered. That testimony revealed that the confessions of Bucher and his crewmen were real enough; that neither fact nor the Code of Conduct were sufficient to prevent Bucher and his crew from making false confessions in the face of physical and mental torture, the severity of which remains unclear. This development led the chairman of the Senate Armed Services Committee Richard Russell to say, "These men are being hailed as heroes. They are heroes in the sense that they survived the imprisonment. But they did sign a great many statements that did not reflect any great heroism in my mind."[13] Included in these statements was a televised one by Bucher in which he described the *Pueblo* mission as a "sheer act of aggression."[14]

In spite of such behavior, public opinion throughout remained highly sympathetic to the *Pueblo* commander and his crew. In February 1968 a Harris poll showed 76 percent of the respondents favoring negotiation to secure release of the *Pueblo* personnel, but four in ten favored

12 Ibid., 24 December 1968, p. 1.
13 Ibid., 31 December 1968, p. 1.
14 Ibid., 29 December 1968, Sec. 4, p. 8.

7

use of force to get the *Pueblo* back and only 2 percent thought that the United States should apologize for spying.[15] In September the American Legion in its annual meeting resolved that if diplomacy failed, the United States should use whatever force was necessary to get the *Pueblo* and its men back.[16] A Remember the *Pueblo* Committee was formed and began to plan demonstrations in November.[17] In March of 1969 it was reported that "at a time when the Armed Forces are perhaps unjustly suspect of an obsolete code of ethics, the wrath of the American public is something the Navy will have to take into account"[18] in determining Bucher's future. Mail pouring in to Congress and the television networks showed the public continued to be supportive of Bucher and his crew and in a protective state of mind.

While the *Pueblo* Court of Inquiry could have recommended to higher authority that Commander Bucher and his men be courtmartialed, such a recommendation could not have been based on a violation of the Code of Conduct. That code has no legal standing and is only a set of guidelines. However, a violation of the code could entail a violation of the Uniform Code of Military Justice, which is law in the full sense where the serviceman is concerned.

The idea of punishing a serviceman who conducts himself improperly before the enemy can be traced in English Law at least as far back as 1672. The first American Articles of War in 1776 carried a provision stating that any soldier who "shall misbehave himself before the enemy" shall suffer death or whatever lesser penalty that may be inflicted.[19] Article 99 of the UCMJ is now titled "Misbehavior before the Enemy." If Bucher and members of the *Pueblo*

15 Ibid., 11 February 1968, p. 9.

16 Ibid., 15 September 1968, p. 23.

17 Ibid., 11 November 1968, p. 62.

18 Alistair Cooke, "Navy Code on Trial at the Pueblo Inquiry," *Louisville Courier-Journal*, 4 March 1969, p. A9.

19 See Peter B. Work, "Misbehavior before the Enemy: A Reassessment," *American Law Review* 17 (July 1968): 447-65.

crew could be shown to have committed acts of cowardice, Article 99 would be applicable and such acts could be punished by death.

Articles 104 and 134 of the UCMJ specify that one who without authorization gives intelligence to or communicates with a known enemy may be punished by death. These two articles were used in gaining court-martial convictions against American prisoners of war during the Korean Conflict. These prisoners made such statements as: The United States conducted biological warfare in Korea; the United States is an illegal aggressor; and the United States Air Force indiscriminantly bombed North Korea. There is some similarity between these statements and those made by members of the *Pueblo* crew. The United States was labeled an aggressor by Bucher and described as the initiator of a spy mission by Lieutenants Harris and Murphy. Eighty-two men of those aboard the *Pueblo* signed a letter to President Johnson calling on him to "frankly admit the fact that we intruded into the territorial waters" of North Korea and to assure North Korea that it would not happen again.[20]

An adequate legal defense for improper communication with an enemy is not easy to establish. In the Korean War cases, the United States Court of Military Appeals (USCMA) held that a violator of these provisions could not legally justify his acts on the grounds that he acted to improve the lot of his compatriots. This decision places the explanations offered by Bucher and others of the *Pueblo* crew in perspective. An adequate defense, the USCMA has said, must show a well-grounded apprehension of immediate and impending death or of immediate, serious, bodily harm to justify unauthorized communication on the ground of coercion or duress.

Finally, Article 92 of the Uniform Code forbids dereliction in the performance of duties and sets as a penalty such punishment as a court-martial may direct. Although semantically, the behavior of the *Pueblo* personnel might have been

20 *New York Times,* 5 March 1968, p. 1.

brought under such provision, the ambiguity surrounding the definition of "duty" in the *Pueblo* situation would probable have encouraged the authorities to utilize other provisions had further prosecution seemed necessary. In any event, it seems clear that while the Code of Conduct is not legally enforceable as an Executive Order, there are legal means of levying punishment on those who violate certain of its provisions. In fact, however, whether the *Pueblo* Court of Inquiry would recommend a court-martial was not solely a legal question. The politics of the situation had to allow for the state of public opinion toward the navy, the *Pueblo* crew, and military justice in general. Public opinion can not only modify a legal decision but in this case seems to have prevented any further legal action against Bucher or his colleagues.

The Court of Inquiry convened by Admiral John H. Hyland completed its deliberations in early May. A number of specific recommendations were made: A general court-martial was recommended for Commander Lloyd Bucher for failing to take "immediate and aggressive" action when the *Pueblo* was first attacked, for permitting the search of his ship while he still had the "power to resist," for following North Korean vessels into port as ordered, for "negligently failing" completely to destroy secret material, and for failing, prior to sailing, to see that the *Pueblo* crew was properly drilled in procedures for destroying secret material under emergency conditions. A general court was also suggested for Lieutenant Stephen Harris for failing effectively to destroy secret gear and for not informing Bucher of unspecified deficiencies in the intelligence section of the *Pueblo*. For Lieutenant Edward Murphy, a letter of admonition was recommended. It was suggested that Murphy might be guilty of failing "to organize and lead the crew on the day of seizure"— especially in regard to the destruction of secret or classified material.[21]

[21] Ibid., 7 May 1969, pp. 1, 24.

The public and the press were somewhat surprised by the recommendations of the court. The sympathy of the public for Bucher and his crew has already been noted. As for the press, most commentators had previously interpreted public concern over the matter as sufficient to discount the probability of further action against *Pueblo* crewmembers. But while the recommendations of the court were surprising, given the politics of the situation, the thrust of earlier speculations in the press turned out to be quite accurate. For on the day that the action of the Court of Inquiry was reported, a superior authority, Secretary of the Navy John H. Chafee, announced that no further action against Commander Bucher and his men would be taken.[22] Chafee did not base his action on the ground that the probability of guilt was so low as to make further prosecution unwarranted. Indeed, he stressed that he was not suggesting in any way that no wrong had been done. However, he said, "they have suffered enough, and further punishment would not be justified." This led a commentator in the *New York Times* to observe that Chafee's action "quite skillfully—perhaps deliberately—blunts this public outcry but, at the same time, hardly exonerates Commander Bucher."[23] In addition it might be observed that Chafee, shunning questions of illegal behavior, chose to let his decision turn on degree of suffering—precisely the kind of value likely to be uppermost in the mind of a layman evaluating the alternatives. This lends enhanced credence to the belief that the decision was politically rather than legally determined.

It is possible to interpret Chafee's action as reflecting (1) the judgment of the executive branch that press reports of public attitudes were accurate, and (2) the sensitivity of the Nixon administration to public opinion. Congress, however, speaks with a different voice. Yet the same considerations appear to have been relevant in shaping a response in the House of Representatives. In July 1969, a subcommit-

22 Ibid.
23 Ibid., p. 24.

tee of the House Armed Services Committee issued a report, after some months of study, heavily critical of the generals and the admirals connected with the *Pueblo* affair. In regard to Bucher and his men, however, the report urged a revision and clarification of the Code of Conduct and suggested that such a revised code should provide some latitude for the behavior required by its provisions. This would seem to validate, at the congressional level, the earlier judgments of the press and the executive branch that public opinion was decidedly against further punishment for the *Pueblo* crewmembers—partly because of the unrealistic behavioral obligations imposed upon them by the 1955 code.

The pro-Bucher feeling of the American people in the *Pueblo* incident also reflects concern with a larger problem—the role of the American citizen in the military culture, the demands made upon him, and the rights accorded him. Whereas the *Pueblo* incident focuses attention on the attempts of the military establishment to control the behavior of the servicemen *vis-à-vis* the enemy, the American public and its representatives have been interested for some time in the other side of the control coin—that which has to do with controlling the behavior of those who prosecute the serviceman for alleged irregularities; or, to put it another way, with the rights of the serviceman who is involved in such a prosecution. In the final analysis, the larger question —the civil, constitutional, and other rights of the serviceman —is of greater significance than the *"Pueblo* incidents" which occasionally dramatize the behavioral expectations held for the serviceman and the treatment accorded him when these expectations are not met. For that reason, and to place these matters in proper perspective, the present study examines the development of American military justice in the context of military prosecutions and the interplay of politics and the public with that development.

One

It is a truism of American politics that Congress and the Supreme Court both respond to the pressures of public opinion. A problem arises, however, in trying to tie particular acts of the Congress or the Court to the opinion of particular publics. Some mitigation of this difficulty is derived from the fact that the Congress and the Court are not equally responsive to all publics. Indeed, response in the area of policy formulation, development, and implementation is more often directed to those publics that "count for something" in the political arena. The publics that count, in turn, are characterized by the presence of large numbers of citizens, influential citizens, or both. If large numbers of voters and influential people coalesce on an issue, it is a foregone conclusion that some policy change will be made by Court, Congress, or both.[24]

One issue about which public opinion has been aroused from time to time revolves around the concept of military justice. While the legal and military professions include specialists who maintain a constant interest in military law, the awareness of other publics in this area is stimulated and most widespread during wartime. Major wars involve massive numbers of citizens. In the early days of the Republic the armed forces numbered 1,000 men. In 1969 it was close to 3,000,000. The larger the number of citizens drafted the more likely the recognition that military and civilian justice differ in many important respects. For large numbers of "amateur" soldiers can be expected to experience the tribulations of court-martial and yet to accept with less equanimity than the professional military man the treatment accorded them.

While the general function of legal systems is to settle disputes and dispense justice, it has been said that military legal systems must be subordinated to winning wars. Or as General William Sherman expressed it, "The object of military law is to govern armies composed of strong men, so as to be capable of exercising the largest measure of force at the will of the Nation."[25] A distinct military law has been maintained in all states of the modern Western world. Indeed, the United States Court of Military Appeals once held that the Military Code enacted in 1951 takes precedence over the federal Constitution insofar as military due process is concerned.[26] Nevertheless, the public or more specifically the nonprofessional military men who have been subjected to the processes of military justice have not always found this "half a loaf" of due process acceptable. Shock and dismay have often been followed by efforts to liberalize military judicial procedures upon the return of the "victim" to civilian life. Since, in general, civilian justice has been more person-oriented than military justice, it would not be surprising if efforts were directed toward equating more closely the rights of military personnel in military courts and civilians in state and federal courts.

While the military profession is apt to argue that some of the problems of the military society call for an expertise which civil judges lack and point to the danger of incorrectly evaluating the effect that a given intrusion on military authority will have on discipline, such arguments tend to lose force when the average adult in this country who

[24] Robert Dahl, "Decision-Making in a Democracy: The Supreme Court as a National Policy Maker," *Journal of Public Law* 6 (1957): 279-95.

[25] John Jay Douglas, "Court Martial Jurisdiction in Future War," *Military Law Review* 25 (Oct. 1960): 48.

[26] *United States* v. *Sutton* 3 U.S.C.M.A. 220; *United States* v. *Jacoby* 11 U.S.C.M.A. 428. Cf. "The Right to Counsel in Special Courts-Martial," *Minnesota Law Review* 50 (1965): 147-69.

reaches draft age can expect to spend 4 percent of his adult life in the armed forces.[27] And the existence of 25 million veterans in the nation provides a sympathetic base of public opinion from which campaigns to liberalize military law may be launched and sustained.

27 Earl Warren, "The Bill of Rights and the Military," *J.A.G. Bulletin* 4 (May-June 1962): 6-21.

Two

Our difficulties stem, in part, from our past. In general, a British heritage has not prevented major changes in procedures and concepts governing the relationships between the individual and his government. The Declaration of Independence focused on the deficiencies of British justice, and our federal and state constitutions establish a number of rights which were unrecognized in contemporary British law.[28] Since the Declaration complained at length about British abuse of certain personal rights, it is not surprising that early state and federal constitutional provisions departed from British practice. It may be recalled, however, that the Declaration also accused George III of attempting to "render the military independent of, and superior to, the civil power."[29] Consequently, the president was made commander in chief of the armed forces and the power to raise, finance, and regulate such forces was given to Congress.

The complaint, however, was two-pronged—it implied that the relationship between military and civil powers should be one of dependence and that the interdependent relationship should be characterized by the subordination of military to civil power. In deciding cases involving the use of military power, the Supreme Court has sometimes felt it necessary to remind us that "the military should always be kept in subjection to the laws of the country to which it belongs," or that "supremacy of the civil over the military is one of our great heritages."[30] But while this principle is subject to dilution in wartime, its inherent strength in our governmental system is beyond doubt, as General Douglas MacArthur learned in his dispute with President Truman over China policy. As a principle, therefore, the superiority of civil to military authority has been maintained throughout the life of the Republic.

In relating the individual to the system of which he is a part, the deviation from British custom and practice seen so clearly in our rules for resolving conflicts in the larger political and social system was not observed initially in the rules adopted for the military subsystem.[31] Thus, in our state and federal courts, we have been moved from the beginning to implement trial by jury, the privilege against

---

28 British law permitted the use of "general warrants" or "writs of assistance" by customs officials. American law has always severely restricted searches and seizures by agents of the state. (General warrants were condemned, however, in *Entick* v. *Carrington*, 19 How. St. Tr. 1029 [1765] and by the House of Commons in a resolution adopted in 1766.) In *Bridges* v. *California*, 314 U.S. 252, the Supreme Court (per Justice Hugo Black) declared: "To assume that English Common Law in this field became ours is to deny the generally accepted historical belief that 'one of the objects of the Revolution was to get rid of the English Common Law on liberty of speech and of the press'. More specifically, it is to forget the environment in which the First Amendment was ratified. In presenting the proposals which were later embodied in the Bill of Rights, James Madison the leader in the preparation of the First Amendment, said: 'Although I know whenever the great rights, the trial by jury, freedom of the press, or liberty of conscience, come in question in that body [Parliament], the invasion of them is resisted by able advocates, yet their Magna Charta does not contain any one provision for the security of those rights, respecting which the people of America are most alarmed. The freedom of the press and rights of conscience, those choicest privileges of the people, are unguarded in the British Constitution'" (pp. 264-65).

29 Approximately twelfth in a list of twenty-five or thirty wrongs cited.

30 *Dow* v. *Johnson*, 10 Otto 158, 169 (Justice Field); *Duncan* v. *Kahanamoku* 327 U.S. 304, 325 (Justice Murphy).

31 That early American statesmen accepted contrary principles for regulating civil and military life cannot be attributed to the fact that diverse individuals were involved in evaluating British practices on the civilian and military sides. The Committee of the Second Continental Congress chosen to revise the 1775 Articles of War consisted of John Adams, Thomas Jefferson, John Rutledge, James Wilson, and R. R. Livingston.

self-incrimination, and the right to counsel.[32] But on the military side, the British recognized no such privileges and we followed their lead without protest by almost literally copying our first Articles of War from the British Code of 1774. The British Code in turn was little changed from the Articles of Richard II adopted in 1385, which were little more than a copy of the principles governing military life in Roman times. Thus, while we can say that civil and military power in the United States have been integrated with military power subordinate, it does not follow that similar sets of principles have operated historically in resolving conflict or dispensing justice in the larger society and in the military subsociety.

[32] While the right against self-incrimination is not mentioned in the Magna Charta, the Petition of Rights, the Bill of Rights, or similar British documents, the privilege was incorporated in the constitutions of seven states prior to 1789 (David Fellman, *The Defendant's Rights* [New York, 1958], p. 154). Similarly, because of the feeling that the benefits of the jury trial were not fully recognized in the colonies, state and federal constitutions incorporated provisions designed to safeguard that right (Art. II, Sec. 2, United States Constitution). The Normans introduced the ordeal of trial by battle—a combat between two litigants to be decided by the "God of Battles." The victor (and the one in the right) was he who put his opponent to death or forced him to concede the battle. The legal right to trial by battle existed in England (if requested) until 1819 or thirty-two years after the framing of the federal Constitution (M. M. Knappen, *Constitutional and Legal History of England* [1964], p. 507).

Three

On the American scene the recent work of the Supreme Court in modifying, formulating, and sustaining the rights of the individual is well known and needs no emphasis. In general that effort has served to broaden the protections granted the individual against state or federal governmental action.[33] We may wonder whether a similar liberalizing trend has occurred in military law, whether the disparity between governing concepts in military and civilian legal systems with which we began our "experiment in democracy" has been maintained, narrowed, or enlarged, and whether doctrinal developments in military law have paralleled, led, or lagged behind similar developments in Supreme Court decision-making.

Our expectations here may be stated as follows: In a political system in which individual preferences are given equal weight, the value of priorities adopted in the system will inevitably encroach upon the variant values of any subsystem involving substantial numbers of citizens who participate in both systems. This follows if a privilege worth preserving in one setting is worth preserving in another. Of course, there may be competing values in the subsystem unique to it, values that lead to giving a fundamental right in the larger system a somewhat lower priority in the smaller. For example, free speech does not establish the right of the serviceman to communicate his critical opinions about the United States to the enemy while a prisoner of war. Yet in civil life, many make political careers out of such assertions. Why the disparity? The

19

answer is simple enough. The military system has as its *raison d'être* the survival of the nation which provides its resources. Where traditional concepts of individual rights touch the raw nerve of security, some restrictions on behavior beyond those that prevail in a civil setting may be anticipated and in many cases defended as reasonable.

The professional soldier understands the need for special restrictions. So does the educated civilian who is familiar with his nation's history. The suspension of civil rights in wartime emergencies is an accepted tradition in this country. While Abraham Lincoln's suspension of habeas corpus during the Civil War and the internment of Japanese-Americans on the West Coast in World War II occasioned some grumbling, there is little question that the great majority of Americans accepted these and similar restrictions as warranted in the context in which they occurred.

[33] This statement runs contrary to one penned by Roscoe Pound in 1921. Writing in the *Harvard Law Review* 21 (Jan. 1921): 1, Pound declared: "What we need to observe is that legal history shows a continual movement back and forth between an extreme solicitude for the general security and the security of social institutions, leading to a minimum of regard for the interests of the individual accused and reliance upon summary, unhampered, arbitrarily administered punitive justice, and at the other extreme excessive solicitude for the social interest in the individual life, leading to a minimum of regard for the general security and security of social institutions and reliance upon strictly regulated judicial punitive justice, hampered at all points by checks and balances and technical obstacles. . . . The exaggerated legalism of nineteenth century administration of the criminal law is being followed hard today by the rise of administrative justice through boards and commissions. The over-technical tenderness for the offender in the nineteenth century is giving way to an overcallousness, to violation of the constitutional rights of accused persons in the supposed interest of efficient enforcement of the penal laws. . . . Excessive securing of the technical rights of accused persons in the nineteenth century produced the third degree just as the excessive zeal of prosecutors, brow-beating of witnesses and unreasonable searches of the seventeenth and eighteenth centuries produced the criminal processes of the nineteenth century" (p. 9).
This strongly Hegelian view does offer a degree of explanation for the "breaks in the curve of individual rights." But, over the long pull, the individual has made progress against the state in carving an inviolable niche for human rights.

When a military system is developed in which primary reliance is placed on temporary citizen-soldiers, either these temporary servicemen must be educated to the realities of military necessity or problems can arise. It is not to be assumed that the millions of draftees brought into service during a war or an emergency period have knowledge or appreciation of all the restrictions on behavior which military life encompasses. These are young men, usually from eighteen to twenty-six years of age. They lack the experience and knowledge of life which their elders possess. They may be insensitive to the nation's historical struggles and the sacrifices these have entailed even though they may have a textbook knowledge of such struggles. Or their analytical powers may not be developed sufficiently for them to grasp the necessity of increased restrictions on individual behavior or of the need for particular restrictions which they find distasteful. Finally, there are probably cases in which individual freedom is needlessly controlled, allowing the careless serviceman to generalize to constraints that serve a more useful purpose.

It seems likely that as large-scale wars call for even larger numbers of these "amateur soldiers," the greater the task of convincing all that the disparities in individual rights between the military and civilian societies are in all cases justified. The legitimacy of curtailing individual privileges and rights beyond the limitations set in civil society is a matter to be established. The larger the numbers of citizen-soldiers, the more difficult this task and the larger the number who will remain unconvinced. In a democratic society, the disappointed have an out. They may make their weight felt in the larger system which in turn may act on the military subsociety to alleviate the complaints and dissatisfactions being voiced. If this process is operative, then we would expect to find the values of the larger system diluting or replacing the variant values of the military system and the legal rights and principles of the soldier approaching more closely those of his civilian counterpart.

As a congressman from South Dakota expressed it in 1919:

Why should not a man placed on trial before a court martial, for murder, for instance, be entitled to just as much protection as he would be entitled to if placed on trial for the same offense before a civil court? The law alleged to be violated is the same, the punishment is the same, and the terrible consequences of the miscarriage of justice are the same. The civil law leaves no stone unturned in building up protection for an accused thus placed in jeopardy. But the military law and the practice under it leave his life to the hazard of what untrained, unskilled, and unadvised army officers may be disposed to do.[34]

Of course, the training and skills of army officers conducting courts-martial have been upgraded drastically since Congressman Royal C. Johnson posed his query. But the question of equal treatment before civil and military law continues to be raised.

To move from the abstract to the concrete, let us consider a specific privilege—the right to counsel in criminal prosecutions—as it has been developed in military and constitutional law. At the same time, we shall give some consideration to the context of other "rights" in which the right to counsel has been developed in military law. Our discussion will be restricted primarily to military law for the army prior to 1951 and for all services thereafter.

The Constitution of 1787 made no provision for the right to counsel in courts of law, but in 1791 the Sixth Amendment, after describing other rights to be secured in criminal prosecutions closed by adding "and to have the assistance of counsel for his defense."[35] This in itself was quite a departure from British practice since, until 1836, the British defendant was denied counsel in felonies though granted such assistance for lesser offenses.[36] While Blackstone com-

[34] Royal C. Johnson, U.S., Congress, House, *Congressional Record*, 65th Cong., 3d sess., 27 February 1919.

[35] Ratified in December 1791.

[36] The consequences of the British practice were sometimes brutal. Although in her native country, Mary, Queen of Scots, would have

plained of this practice, William M. Beaney has suggested that since criminal defendants were enemies of the king, the prevailing view was one of probable guilt, and doubts about the matter were more likely to be resolved in the king's favor if the defendant were deprived of counsel.[37] After 1836 British defendants were able to retain counsel, and after 1903 committing magistrates and judges of assize were permitted to appoint counsel for indigent defendants under certain conditions.

---

been entitled to six advocates, she was denied counsel in the English courts even though English was not her native tongue. And in the 1740s' trial of Simon Lord Lovat in the House of Lords, counsel were not permitted to examine defense witnesses or to cross-examine those for the prosecution. This led Lovat to plead with the court: "My lords, I have not had the use of my limbs these three years: I cannot see, I cannot hear; and I beg, if your lordships have a mind I should have any chance for my life, that you will allow either my counsel or solicitors to examine my witnesses, and to cross-examine those produced on behalf of the crown, and to take notes."

Whereupon the Lord High Steward replied: "It is my duty to acquaint your lordship with what is the known and clear law in these cases . . . by the known rules of law in proceedings of this kind, they [your counsel] have not liberty to assist you in matters of fact, or in the examination of witnesses." Without such assistance, Lovat was adjudged guilty of treason, the Court declaring: "That you, Simon Lord Lovat, return to the prison of the Tower, from whence you came; from thence you must be drawn to the place of execution; when you come there, you must be hanged by the neck, but not till you are dead; for you must be cut down alive; then your bowels must be taken out, and burnt before your face; then your head must be severed from your body, and your body divided into four quarters; and these must be at the king's disposal. And God Almighty be merciful to your soul!" (18 How. St. Tr. 529, [1747]).

Grant has referred to this as judicial murder and perhaps it was that (J. A. C. Grant, *Our Common Law Constitution* [1960], p. 8). But the harshness of the "murder" was diluted somewhat, since the methods outlined by the court for executing the sentence were not followed in putting Lovat to death in 1746. He suffered no worse a fate than beheading on the executioner's block.

37 William M. Beaney, *The Right to Counsel in American Courts* (Ann Arbor, Mich., 1955), p. 11.

Four

The earlier British practices undoubtedly influenced the adoption by the states of the right to counsel in criminal cases. By 1787 all eleven states had recognized such a right in fairly broad terms in constitution or statutes. South Carolina, as early as 1731, provided for court-appointed counsel in capital cases if the accused would be undefended otherwise.[38] Consequently, the adoption of the right in the Sixth Amendment broke no new ground—it emphasized a principle already widely approved. The meaning of the federal principle, however, remained to be established. In the 1789 Judiciary Act[39] and the 1790 Federal Crimes Act,[40] Congress lent its hand to that task. In the former, the Congress that adopted the Sixth Amendment provided that litigants in federal courts might retain counsel, but did not provide for appointing them. In the latter, Congress required that counsel be appointed in all capital cases in federal courts if the defendant so requested. Yet, sixteen years later when the new government revised the Articles of War for the first time, no right to counsel was written into military law.

The 1806 Articles specified general and regimental or garrison courts for trying violations of law by military personnel.[41] The general court-martial consisted of five to thirteen commissioned officers, with the higher number required if available. These courts were appointed by the general commanding an army or the colonel commanding a department. The regimental or garrison court in contrast consisted of three commissioned officers appointed by the officer commanding a regiment or a corps. The regimental courts were permitted to try noncapital cases and noncommissioned personnel. They were restricted to meting out fines not in excess of one month's pay and imprisonment of one month or less. The general court tried all serious offenses and could levy the death sentence under appropriate circumstances. Some distinction of this kind has been maintained to this day, since the general court continues to handle the more serious violations of law and its judgment against defendants is usually more deprivational.

A consequence of the higher cost for the individual of a negative judgment by a general court-martial was a greater emphasis on procedural protections against a miscarriage of justice. While the general court could pass a death sentence, certain restrictions were imposed upon the court in making and executing such a decision. In the first place, the sentence required a two-thirds vote of the court. Moreover, such sentences could not be executed without approval of the convening authority in time of war. In time of peace, no man could be put to death without the added approval of the secretary of war and the president.

In addition to the distinction between courts, the 1806 Articles maintained the traditional distinctions between officers and nonofficers. This was seen in the right of all officers to be tried by a general court. Moreover, in time of war general officers sentenced to death rated review of the sentence by the secretary of war and the president. Even in the general court-martial, officers had the right not to be tried by officers of inferior rank. If charged with an offense,

38 Grant, *Our Common Law Constitution*, p. 10.

39 1 Stat. 92 (1789).

40 2 Stat. 118 (1790): In capital offenses, every person "shall also be allowed and admitted to make his full defense by counsel learned in the law; and the court before whom such person shall be tried, or some judge thereof, shall, and they are hereby authorized and required immediately upon his request to assign to such person such counsel, not exceeding two, as such person shall desire, to whom such counsel shall have free access at all seasonable hours."

41 2 Stat. 359 (April 10, 1806).

an officer was confined to quarters, whereas nonofficers were stockaded.

A third feature of the 1806 system was the recognition of a number of individual rights similar to those prevailing in civilian court systems. No military trials were to be conducted except between the hours of 8:00 A.M. and 3:00 P.M., with certain exceptions. Neither officers nor nonofficers were to be confined more than eight days without being tried, or until such time as a court could be assembled. Officers and provost marshals were required to make out reports within twenty-four hours after prisoners were committed to their charge, such reports going to the commanding officer and stating the name of the prisoner, his crime, and the name of the officer who committed him. Failure to comply with this regulation was, in itself, punishable by court-martial. No court was allowed to impose more than fifty lashes. Double jeopardy was forbidden. No soldier could be tried more than two years after his crime unless he had been a fugitive for a longer period; and he could be tried only by general court-martial. If the prisoner stood mute, he was to be treated as if he had pleaded innocence. And the right of the prisoner to challenge members of the court-martial was recognized. Some of these provisions would be viewed as progressive indeed in view of recent efforts by the Supreme Court to eliminate the incommunicado detention of those accused of criminal acts, and the procedures in some states which traditionally permitted judge and prosecutor to comment unfavorably on the failure of a defendant to take the stand in his defense.

All this suggests that the Congress in 1806 recognized some of the procedural principles governing trials in the civilian legal system as having validity in the military subsystem. However, right to counsel was not one of these. Or at least, it was one considered of less value in the military system than the principles against double jeopardy, cruel and unusual punishment, or incommunicado detention. On the other hand, the prosecutor for the government

—the judge advocate—was instructed to provide some "counsel-type" assistance to an accused in Article 69 of the code. That Article declared that "The Judge Advocate, or some person deputed by him, or by the general or officer commanding the Army, detachment, or garrison, shall prosecute in the name of the United States, but shall so far consider himself as counsel for the prisoner, and after the said prisoner shall have made his plea, as to object to any leading question to any of the witnesses, or any questions to the prisoner, the answer to which might tend to incriminate himself." This provision had been inserted in the previously adopted British Articles by the Continental Congress. Although this lumping of prosecutorial and defense functions in the same person violates certain principles dear to lawyers, the Article did assert the right of a military defendant against self-incrimination. The effectiveness of such a safeguard, under the procedures outlined, is questionable. For not only was a conflict of interests inherent in such arrangements, but conflicts between prosecution and defense interests were likely to be resolved in favor of the prosecution. This follows from the dependence of the judge advocate on his superiors for career advancement.

Five

Further revisions of procedural guarantees for defendants in courts-martial occurred in 1874.[42] In 1806 a general court could be appointed by either a general officer or a colonel commanding a department. In 1874, this authority was restricted to general officers. In addition, a stipulation was added that when the general officer was the accuser or prosecutor of any officer under his command, the court was to be appointed by the president, with its proceedings and sentence being sent directly to the secretary of war and then to the president for final approval or orders in the case.

Article 80 of the new code provided, in time of war, for a field officer to be designated in every regiment to try soldiers for noncapital offenses. The same Article prohibited the use of a regimental or garrison court-martial when a field officer of one's regiment could be detailed. New restrictions were imposed upon permissible punishment. Penitentiary confinement was not to be allowed unless such punishment was allowed for the same offense committed in violation of some statute of the United States, state, territory, or district or by common law.

During Roman times the practice of branding was common. It was the habit to burn a "D" on the hips or buttocks of deserters. Bad characters were branded with the letters "BC." In the United States, habitual drunkards were branded "HD," mutineers "M," cowards "C." "I" was used for insubordination and "W" for worthlessness. Sometimes these letters were tattooed and as late as the Civil War, branding and tattooing were carried out on the cheeks and the head as well as the hip. All such "uncivilized" acts seem to have ended about 1872. But they were not forbidden by the Articles of War until the 1874 revision. Article 98 of the revised code flatly prohibited the punishment of any person in the military service by flogging, branding, marking, or tattooing on the body.

Finally, the 1874 revision retained the responsibility of the judge advocate to military prisoners subject to prosecution. Although the language used is almost literally carried over from the 1806 Code, some expansion in meaning occurred in practice.

By 1874 the privilege of counsel was interpreted to mean that the judge advocate or his delegate was to exercise "paternal-like" care over a military defendant, particularly when such a defendant was an enlisted man.[43] The accused was not to be allowed to suffer because of ignorance or misconception of his legal rights. While voluntary confessions and pleas of guilty were admitted, it was considered improper for the judge advocate to counsel the defendant to plead guilty.[44] Still, the legal rights of the defendant in a military court were severely limited. While it appears that such courts sometimes permitted the employment of counsel, the military man had no such statutory right in 1874 and military courts had no authority to assign counsel to a prisoner.[45] From 1806 to 1874, whatever the practice might have been, Congress found no reason to enlarge the right of the military defendant to have assistance of counsel in defending himself.

As for the enlargement of other rights, the 1874 changes are not impressive. The revisions do reflect some concern over the nature of punishments and the objectivity of General Courts. But one is forced to conclude that in the

42 18 Stat. 228 (1874).

43 After 1874 a judge advocate was required to be appointed by the convening authority for all general courts-martial.

44 R. A. Ives, *A Treatise on Military Law* (New York, 1881), p. 230.

45 Opinion of Judge Advocate General 200 (1880).

sixty-eight years preceding the new enactment the thinking of Congress in this area changed little if at all. The patronizing tone of the 1806 Code is equally present in that of 1874. The view that procedure in military courts was subordinate to the need for discipline went unchallenged on the whole. Such a view, however, was quite contemporary in the Western world, however unenlightened it might appear today.

On the civilian side, the Supreme Court was similarly inactive. The right of the federal defendant to employ counsel and to have counsel appointed in capital cases existed from 1790 and contrasts with the much more limited concern of Congress with the defense of accused military personnel. Why this should be so is not at all clear. The Sixth Amendment did not require, initially, that counsel be appointed for indigent defendants in capital cases. Congress reflected its own values (and possibly those of the community) when it legislated the right. Presumably, there would be no less concern with finding truth in a military court than in a nonmilitary one. If counsel could assist in that process in one case, why not in the other? It is to be assumed that the interest in avoiding mistaken convictions would be of equal weight in both settings. On the assumption that counsel is a protection against such mistakes, their employment in one setting but not in the other seems incongruous.

Since the congressional legislation applied to federal courts only, the states were free to pursue their own whims in this area. While the right to counsel was assured in many state constitutions, it is safe to say that the right, in general, was considerably more restricted than in federal courts. The Supreme Court made no serious effort to interfere with state restrictions on the right until 1932.

The failure of the Court to take effective action between 1806 and 1874 was undoubtedly a consequence of the existence of the congressional statutes and the absence of sophisticated pressure for expansion of the right. On the other hand, the failure of the Court to enlarge the privilege of counsel and other protections for the individual before a court-martial stemmed from its posture *vis-à-vis* the military establishment. The Court's conservative stance on the question of civil-military relations was starkly illustrated by its decisions in *Ex parte Vallandigham*[46] and *Dynes* v. *Hoover*[47] that the judgment of a military tribunal is not subject to direct review by a civil court.

[46] 1 Wallace 243.
[47] 20 Howard 65.

Six

In 1916 Congress legislated a third revision of the Articles of War.[48] In this version we encounter a threefold division of courts-martial into general, special, and summary courts. The general court is equated with that provided for in 1806; the special court replaced the regimental or garrison court; and the summary court, consisting of one officer, replaced the field officer designation or field court established in 1874. Whereas in 1874 only general officers could appoint general courts, in 1916 this authority was delegated to the president and various commanding officers down to the brigade level. This change could be viewed as negative for individual rights, since it enlarged the number of persons who could decide to bring serious charges against an accused. Other provisions were more positive. The appointment of special and summary courts were restricted to commanding officers. An important new protection was provided in that no officer could sit as a member of a general or special court if he was the accuser or a witness for the prosecution. In addition, each general or special court required the appointment of a judge advocate and, in the case of the latter, one or more assistant judge advocates were necessary.

The jurisdiction of the general court remained sufficiently broad to cover any person subject to military law who committed a crime or offense made punishable by the Articles. The special court was limited to offenses against military law of a noncapital nature excluding commissioned officers. The special court was also barred from handing down a dishonorable discharge and was limited to meting out sentences of six months or less or to a forfeiture of pay of six months or less. The jurisdiction of the summary court was the most restrictive. It was given power to try any person subject to military law excluding commissioned officers and several other categories of servicemen. A maximum sentence available in a summary court was three months confinement or a forfeiture of three months pay. In the case of both the special and summary courts, the president was authorized to exempt from the jurisdiction of these courts any class or classes of persons subject to military law. And noncommissioned officers were given the privilege of refusing to be tried by a summary court-martial unless such court had been convened upon the authority of an officer competent to bring them before a general court-martial.

Article 17 of the 1916 Code reflected a greater concern with the right to counsel in general and special courts-martial. The accused was specifically given the right to be represented before such courts by counsel of his own selection if such counsel was reasonably available. In the event that he was unrepresented, the judge advocate was obligated throughout the proceedings to advise the accused of his legal rights. Compulsory self-incrimination was specifically prohibited by Article 24. Article 40 repeated the earlier prohibition against double jeopardy. Interest in fair trial procedures was maintained and slightly broadened. Upon being arrested for the purpose of trial, the accused was to be provided with a copy of the charges against him within eight days. The trial itself was required to be held within ten days unless the necessities of the service prevented such action. In the event that a copy of the charges was not served or the arrested person was not brought to trial within the stipulated period, the arrest was to be nullified and the accused released from custody. But in a strange twist, a proviso was added which allowed the service

48 39 Stat. 650.

to rearrest and try the released individual, whenever the exigencies of the service permitted, within twelve months after being released.

In these changes, we detect some interest in improving the objectivity of those who sat as judges in court-martial proceedings; in safeguarding the rights of an accused between arrest and trial; and in providing greater protection for the individual during trial by explicitly granting the right to counsel of his own choosing where possible. At the same time, the code left unclear the question of military versus civilian counsel as well as questions concerning the cost of such services and who was to bear them. These omissions may be explained in part by two factors: One was the practice of granting certain nonstatutory rights to servicemen by army order; the second had to do with the primary motivation for the code changes. In testifying before a Senate subcommittee in 1916, General Enoch H. Crowder said:

It is now the rule rather than the exception that an accused person is represented before a court-martial by counsel of his own selection, either civil or military. [In spite of assumptions in the Articles of War to the contrary] Since 1890 orders have imperatively required the demand of the accused for military counsel to be met, except in the single instance where the individual officer desired by an accused was not available. In the case where an accused is represented by counsel of his own selection the law should not impose upon the judge advocate any part of the counsel's duties; and clearly where the accused is unrepresented by the counsel the judge advocate should be required to look after and safeguard all his legal rights and not two of them.[49]

While this statement was perhaps encouraging and showed some progress from earlier days, the practice guaranteed little. Indeed, several senators raised the point specifically in the hearing and were told by General Crowder that he, personally, had no objection to requiring the procedure then in use by statute rather than by army order. That this

[49] U.S., Congress, Senate, *Report #106*, 64th Cong., 1st sess., 7 February 1916, p. 41.

was not adequately accomplished in the final version of the legislation relates directly to the second and primary factor behind the proposed changes in the Articles.

The impetus for the new legislation came from the army and other defense forces in the United States. The move was motivated by certain conditions revealed in the Mexican War, the Spanish–American War, and in "colonial" possessions such as the Panama Canal Zone, that is, questions of the jurisdiction of the army over certain crimes of soldiers and camp followers not then covered. At the same time it was politic to suggest the need to alleviate some of the procedural shortcomings and severe penalties available or required under the 1874 Articles. And it is possible that some army leaders were sincerely interested in this latter problem. In any event, it was hoped that the revisions could be made as the chairman of the Senate Military Affairs Committee, George E. Chamberlain, put it, "without any very radical changes in the Articles of War that have been in force since before the beginning of the last century."[50]

Article 92 of the 1916 Articles granted the army its major goal, that is, jurisdiction over the crimes of rape and murder committed by military personnel outside the United States. But the new code also adhered to Senator Chamberlain's thought that no major systemic changes were necessary or requested. Or, as a former judge advocate general of the army analyzed the congressional action: "It did nothing but assemble, classify and render more convenient old articles, dressed them up in rather more modern language, wrote into them what hitherto had been legally implied into them by construction, and made not one single fundamental change."[51]

Thus, on the eve of United States entry into World War I, the prevailing system of military justice was characterized

50 U.S., Congress, Senate, *Congressional Record*, 64th Cong., 1st sess., 24 July 1916, p. 11511.

51 S. T. Ansell, "Military Justice," *Cornell Law Quarterly* 5 (Nov. 1919): 4.

primarily by the army's view of military law. The philosophy that military justice should be controlled by the power of military command remained dominant. The court-martial was viewed as an executive agency belonging to and under control of the military commander. This was not an excessive description given the fact that the commander, under the procedures existing in 1916, exercised almost unlimited discretion in deciding who should be charged, the sufficiency of evidence, the composition of the court, questions of law, and other procedural questions arising during court-martial proceedings. The thought that military commanders must have absolute control in order to maintain discipline was undoubtedly the prevailing one. Consequently, it was not only unobjectionable but necessary for the commander to perform judicial, legislative, and executive functions in disciplinary proceedings affecting those under his command. The relationship of this perspective to principles of civil law was spelled out in 1912 by the judge advocate general of the army who, before a congressional committee, described military law as a departure from civil law which should not be sacrificed to principles of civil jurisprudence.[52]

The army also had its "civilian" defenders. In 1919 John Henry Wigmore argued that "The prime object of military organization is Victory, not Justice. The Army's object is to kill, disable, or capture our enemy before he can kill or capture us. In that death-struggle which is ever impending, the Army, which defends the Nation, is strained by the terrific consciousness that the Nation's life and its own is every moment at stake. No other objective than Victory can have first place in its thoughts; there is never any remission of that strain. If the Army can do Justice to its men, well and good. But Justice is always secondary; and Victory is always primary."[53]

[52] Ibid., p. 7.
[53] John Henry Wigmore, "Lessons from Military Justice," *Journal of the American Judicature Society* 4 (Dec. 1920): 151-57.

Taken out of context, this statement is somewhat over-done, for while an armed force must give victory a higher priority than justice and when they are polar opposites choose the former, in reality victory and justice are seldom, if ever, opposites. Indeed, victory implies morale and morale, justice. Therefore an army must always be concerned with justice in the broad sense.

More disagreement may be occasioned in regard to the details of implementation. But Wigmore argued correctly that in many ways military justice was superior to civilian justice.[54] He observed, for example, that a record of every general court-martial was kept and forwarded to the judge advocate general in Washington for review. This guaranteed appellate review of all such cases, a privilege lacking in the civil system. He noted that the verbatim record of all general courts-martial was not duplicated on the civil side, that only two states possessed minimum indeterminate sentence laws, a principle which characterized military procedures, and that psychiatric examination of accused persons before trial was much more prevalent in the military system than in the civil.

More critical views were based primarily upon the assumption that civil and military procedures, particularly those designed to protect individual defendants, should be substantially similar or that military justice should be regulated by established principles of law. This was not, however, a view supported by Congress, the nation's press, or its leading statesmen and opinion makers. Additional evidence was needed to make this position more persuasive. Certain events that transpired in France and elsewhere during United States participation in World War I provided the necessary impetus for and development of cogent arguments for reform of the military judicial system.

Subsequent to the interpretations of the Sixth Amendment in the Congressional Statutes of 1789 and 1790, there is no further authoritative guidance to its meaning until

54 Ibid., passim.

1938. There was no common-law precedent requiring the appointment of counsel except in treason cases. In 1874 the general understanding was that the right in noncapital cases consisted of the privilege of employing counsel in federal courts if the prisoner could afford it. In 1916 the understanding remained essentially the same. But as William M. Beaney points out, federal courts possessed and exercised the power to appoint counsel in serious cases that were less than capital.[55] Such practices occasionally involved the Supreme Court prior to *Johnson* v. *Zerbst*.[56] In 1898 the Court upheld an appointment of counsel by a federal judge against a charge of discrimination. But between 1898 and 1916 Beaney reports no cases involving the right to counsel. Thus between 1806 and 1916, the slight enlargement of the privilege which occurred in the Articles of War was not matched by activity in this area by the Supreme Court.

The federal lower courts, on the other hand, were somewhat beyond the military courts, since, on their own initiative, they occasionally appointed counsel for defendants in noncapital cases. It is clear in this period that military courts occasionally appointed counsel for military defendants. But the *ad hoc* practices of courts, military or otherwise, at their discretion, is not to be equated with the rights of accused to counsel as stated in the Sixth Amendment, congressional legislation, and authoritative announcements by the Supreme Court.

We can say then that by 1916, the right of the defendant in a federal criminal trial to have counsel furnished in capital cases was a legal right which did not exist in military courts. We can say further that the lower federal courts evidenced a slightly higher degree of sensitivity to the importance of counsel to fair trial than Congress reflected in its enactments and revisions of the Articles of War. But in neither case, by modern standards, are we likely to be impressed by the practices in this area up to 1916.

[55] Beaney, *The Right to Counsel in American Courts*, p. 41.
[56] 304 U.S. 458.

Seven

During the period April 6, 1917, to June 30, 1919, 145 death penalties were handed down by military courts-martial. Execution was consummated in thirty-five; ten in France and twenty-five in the United States.[57] Additional thousands of American troops were subjected to military detention and court-martial procedures which left many of them aghast. Soldiers' complaints do not necessarily establish a basis for fundamental changes as opposed to procedural changes in military legal practices. Nor can we evaluate with certainty all the allegations made by those who expressed their dissatisfactions. But these are not the critical questions. The focal issues are the nature and magnitude of the complaints and the extent to which Congress was moved to act as a result of them.

The allegations made were indeed serious. Cruelties were alleged to have been practiced against American soldiers by the provost marshal's force in Paris. It was claimed that military prisoners were beaten, clubbed, starved, thrown into prison without trial and without charges being preferred against them. Reports that the regular army mistreated soldiers from the National Guard were circulated. Brigadier General W. W. Harts, who was in command of American military forces in the Paris area during the war and later, was ordered home to answer charges that "strong-armed, 'hard-boiled', bloodthirsty police companies swept the streets of Paris making wholesale arrests of American soldiers."[58] Hart denied such charges before Congress claiming they were exaggerated by men seeking to exculpate themselves. He suggested that many of these men were "skulkers"[59] who did not wish to remain with their divisions at the front. Colonel Edgar P. Grinstead, who commanded an American prison farm at Challes, France, during the war, reported that "Everybody that was a soldier in France knew that thousands of our men were running away from the front lines, and that had the war continued many executions would have been necessary before these desertions could have been stopped."[60] At the same time, the *New York Times* editorially suggested that the complaining soldiers were probably stretching the truth. Said the *Times,* "To be remembered, too, is the fact that all of these witnesses belong to a class the members of which are not models of military propriety."[61]

57 *New York Times,* 28 November 1919, p. 14.

58 Ibid., 7 April 1920, p. 9. Other atrocities against American soldiers were reported. Congressman Frederick W. Dallinger of Massachusetts reported allegations made to him that "our own loved ones were beaten, clubbed, starved—all in the name of democracy; that men caught in the web of the American military police system of Paris were placed in prison pens viler than those of Andersonville; that our soldiers, some of them wearing wound stripes, some returned to duty after weeks and months of suffering in hospitals, were thrown into prison without trial and without charges ever being preferred against them for such offenses as failure to have proper military travel orders in their possession. Evidence is produced showing that men were hit and clubbed until they bled and fainted, and that one man even preferred death to the treatment to which he was subjected, and took his own life" (*New York Times,* 13 July 1919, p. 1).

The quantity of such reports led Representative Thomas D. Schall of Minnesota to introduce a joint resolution in the House of Representatives recommending a presidential pardon for all persons who, while in the military during World War I, were convicted by courts-martial for offenses not involving moral turpitude (*New York Times,* 23 May 1920, p. 13). It was reported in the *Times* of 16 July 1919 that food was so scarce in American prison camps that the men ate potato peels (p. 13); and that regular army personnel grossly mistreated their compatriots from the National Guard (*New York Times,* 21 July 1919, p. 10).

59 In responding to reports that soldiers under his command sold "rights" in the Paris subway to Frenchmen, Hart said that he personally investigated the charge and found it to be true. The soldier in question, however, denied that he sold one of the bridges over the Seine River to a Frenchman (*New York Times,* 13 April 1920, p. 20).

60 *New York Times,* 1 August 1919, p. 15.

But during our brief involvement in the war, several hundred thousand soldiers were court-martialed. Most of these men were "citizen soldiers" who had no qualms at all about complaining to their congressmen. These complaints had an effect. In March 1919 Congressman Dan V. Stephens stated in the House of Representatives, "It is conceded on all sides that courts-martial procedure during the present war has been atrociously harsh, brutal and unjust. There is hardly a Member of Congress who has not directly received convincing evidence of that fact through innumerable justified complaints from his constituency, establishing beyond all doubt that courts-martial are not worthy the name of courts."[62]

In the same month, a group of lawyers recently returned from service in the judge advocate general's department of the army issued a statement to the press charging that "The present system of military justice is a system of practiced injustice. We are lawyers who were commissioned as officers in Judge Advocate General Crowder's department. We were amazed and shocked by the court-martial system. We found that it secures no adequate protection of men charged with military crimes; it permits the conviction and punishment of innocent men, as well as the imposition of unduly harsh sentences upon men who have been guilty of trivial offenses."[63]

A month earlier, Congressman Royal C. Johnson informed the House, "I have seen injustice in the Army. The existing military code does not establish and guarantee justice to the enlisted man of the Army. I will speak more strongly than that. If followed, in many cases it does not permit of justice. The code and the procedure under it are offensive to any enlightened sense of natural justice, and equally offensive to those fundamental principles of law

61 19 July 1919, p. 8.

62 Appendix to U.S., Congress, House, *Congressional Record*, 65th Cong., 3d sess., 3 March 1919, p. 279.

63 *New York Times*, 28 March 1919, p. 12.

which are elemental in our institutions and which reflect our civilization."[64]

At the same time, defense authorities seemed reluctant to admit the charges or to prosecute those responsible. Eventually several courts-martial were initiated to punish the officers guilty of brutality to American prisoners in France. But of the two most notorious cases, that of Lieutenant "Hard Boiled" Smith and Captain Carl Detzer, the outcomes were not welcomed by the critics of the system. Smith was convicted and served four months while Detzer was acquitted. In the latter case, Detzer was charged with twenty-eight counts. The allegations included forcing prisoners to swallow lighted cigarettes, striking them with his fist, and forcing confessions. Not only was Detzer found not guilty but the court deliberated only ten minutes. This led the *New York Times* to editorialize that Detzer's acquittal could only mean that the prosecution witnesses had perjured themselves.[65]

The Detzer case was important for two reasons. Ironically, the trial revealed the inadequacy of protections for the military defendant even before a general court. In questioning Detzer, the trial judge advocate became so vigorous that a member of the court objected that the questions were incriminating and that the prisoner was not being allowed to answer. The court proceeded to overrule this objection from one of its own members. Later, however, the court was obliged to reprimand the trial judge advocate for implying that Detzer had behaved cowardly in the face of a pistol threat by a soldier he was attempting to arrest. These proceedings pointed up the need for a greater sensitivity in *military* courts to the principles of law governing prosecution in *civil* courts.

Second, the outcome did not satisfy those attacking the system and hence did nothing to diminish the demands

64 U.S., Congress, House, *Congressional Record*, 65th Cong., 3d sess., 27 February 1919, p. 4503.

65 *New York Times,* 10 February 1920, p. 8.

being made on the Congress. All those who favored reform could not be dismissed as "crackpots" or "soreheads." One of the leaders in the reform movement was Samuel T. Ansell, who had served as acting judge advocate general during the War. Eventually the great cacaphony led to investigations by a special War Department Board, by a committee of the American Bar Association, and by Congress. The War Department Board found the "lack of competent trial judge advocates and counsel" to be a major weakness and recommended that defense counsel be appointed for such general and special courts-martial and that young officers be offered specific inducements to study law.[66] In general, however, the board recommended that the system remain relatively unchanged remarking that "courts-martial have always been agencies for creating and maintaining the discipline of armies" rather than agencies for the "nice exemplification of technical rules of law."[67] This position was supported by Secretary of War Newton Baker.

The committee of the American Bar Association took a similar position by a majority vote.[68] This led the chairman of the committee, Samuel T. Ansell, to charge that the committee was partisan—that it tended to interview witnesses favorable to the existing system and to ignore opponents.[69] In July 1919 Ansell resigned from the army and continued his efforts for reform. This he was able to do as counsel for the House Investigating Committee which was established to look into the matter of brutality in the prison camps. In September, former President William Howard Taft, in a copyrighted newspaper article, came out strongly for the prevailing system of military justice.[70] The Taft article provided Ansell with additional opportunity to press a favorite theme. In so doing, he raised the brouhaha

66 Ibid., 25 August 1919, p. 1.
67 Ibid.
68 Ibid., 28 July 1919, p. 7.
69 Ibid.
70 Ibid., 16 September 1919, p. 4.

to a more general, intellectual, and theoretical level. In late 1919 Ansell wrote General Leonard Wood that "Never again can or will we fight a great war with an army of American citizens subjected to a system of discipline that was designed for the Government of the professional military serfs of another age and utterly unsuited to the armies of citizens called to the national defense."[71] A month later, in responding to Taft, Ansell asserted that Taft "turns his back upon the whole theory of a citizen army."[72]

The distinction between a citizen army and a professional

[71] Ibid., 4 August 1919, p. 2.

[72] Ansell's reply to a former president was a strong one, indeed. He wrote: Taft "approves the shocking injustices done to our soldiers during the war. He approves the shameful fact that in the year preceding the armistice 28,000 men were tried by general courts-martial, and 35,000 by inferior courts-martial out of an army that averages less than two million. He approves the fact that men were executed in the dawn following the last day of trial and without the records of their cases ever having been reviewed as the laws of Congress require; executed so summarily, that the executed had no time even to apply to the President for a pardon, or to compose their affairs. He approves the fact that discipline, so called, was obtained . . . through methods of terrorization. He approves the thousands of cases where our men were sentenced for trivial offenses to life long imprisonment. He approves the shockingly harsh sentences averaging, including the most trivial offenses, confinement for seven years. He approves the brutality that has been practiced upon our soldiery in the prison camps both in France and at home. He approves the fistic enforcement of discipline" (*New York Times,* 16 September 1919, p. 4). In reporting Ansell's comments on Taft, we intend no implications regarding their validity. Ansell's letter does illustrate the depth of his emotional commitment to the need for changes in certain military practices in his day. As for Ansell's charges in general, it is worth noting that a major critic, the *Chicago Tribune,* in commenting on Ansell's testimony before the United States Senate did not charge him with false statement. An editorial of 15 February 1919 did challenge Ansell's judgment, saying: "General Ansell's testimony . . . is based on a fundamental misconception. He thinks the first object of an army is justice. It is not. The first object of an army is victory." When a congressman from Missouri criticized the insertion of the editorial in the *Congressional Record,* he was interrupted with applause five times in a statement occupying only sixty lines of print in the *Record* (U.S., Congress, House, *Congressional Record,* 65th Cong., 3d sess., 27 February 1919, p. 4508). This would seem to reflect the feeling of many representatives regarding the charges made.

one had not loomed large in the minds of military and other leaders who, while admitting some abuses by certain individuals, saw little fundamentally wrong with the system as it then existed. However, in terms of the emphasis which political theory in the United States has always placed on the dignity and rights of the individual, the concern of Ansell was basic. This is not meant to imply that the principles of organization and discipline should be distinct. These principles are determined more by the goals of armies than by the social variations of their human components. However, armies cannot be completely insensitive to the expectations of their cadre and the procedures for governing the hardened trooper may be ill suited for the youthful draftee. To the extent that armies can take such differences into account without seriously jeopardizing their primary function, it would seem the better part of valor to do so. This suggests some greater attention to the civil rights of the serviceman beyond those that armies historically have given.

In 1919, then, we find a system of military regulation basically unchanged since 1775 but under intense fire for specific abuses with lapses on the part of the military spotlighting discrepancies between the rights of American draftees in the armed forces and citizens in general. This discrepancy was not able for long to survive the political pressures created by numerous and enlightened critics.

Eight

In April 1920 the Senate Military Affairs Committee reported a bill designed to alter drastically the 1916 Articles of War—the stated aim being to improve the system of military justice.[73] Although the War Department Board was not happy with the proposals, major portions of the bill were enacted into law in the same year.

In the 1920 revision,[74] general, special, and summary courts-martial were retained in essentially the same form, with the general court to consist of any number of officers not less than five as compared to the earlier provision for some number between five and thirteen. A significant innovation required the convening authority to appoint a trial judge advocate and a defense counsel for each general or special court-martial, and one or more assistant trial judge advocates and one or more assistant defense counsel for each general court-martial when necessary. In addition, officers who acted as members, trial judge advocates, assistant trial judge advocates, defense counsel, or assistant defense counsel in any case were barred subsequently from acting as staff judge advocate to reviewing or confirming authority upon the same case.

Certain changes were made in the jurisdictional statement of the several courts and in the punishment available at each of the three levels. An important change permitted an officer competent to appoint a general court for the trial in any case to cause such case to be tried by a special court if, in his judgment, it was in the interest of the service to do so. In such a situation a limitation upon the jurisdiction of the special court as to offenses was to be set aside, but the limitations upon jurisdiction as to persons and punishing power were to be observed. Special courts were further restricted in regard to forfeiture of pay and punishing power.

The right of an accused to counsel was expanded in Article 17. Under the 1920 revision, the accused was granted the right to be represented in his defense before a general or special court by counsel of his own selection, civil counsel if he so provided, or military counsel where such was reasonably available. Otherwise, representation by the defense counsel duly appointed by the court was to be granted. In the event that the accused had counsel of his own selection, the defense counsel and assistant defense counsel of the court, would, if the accused so desired, act as the defendant's associate counsel.

Protections against self-incrimination and double jeopardy were retained but, as for double jeopardy, Article 40 permitted trial a second time for the same offense granted that the accused consented. The earlier prohibition against flogging, branding, marking, or tattooing on the body was enlarged by prohibiting cruel and unusual punishments of every kind. A further restriction on sentencing added to the unanimity requirement for the death sentence and the two-thirds requirement applicable to certain questions in general and special courts, the requirement that no sentence of more than ten years imprisonment be made without the concurrence of three-fourths of all the members present at the time the vote was taken. Otherwise, all questions were to be determined by a majority vote. Where the court had discretion as to sentence, other limitations upon punishment could be prescribed by the president. And in time of peace the confinement period in the penitentiary was not to exceed the maximum period prescribed by law.

To obtain greater flexibility in correcting mistakes that

73 *New York Times,* 17 April 1920, p. 19.
74 41 Stat. 787.

might occur in the dispensation of military justice, a Board of Review consisting of three officers was established in the office of the judge advocate general (JAG). All cases subject to presidential confirmation were first to be approved by the board and the JAG. The Board of Review, in conjunction with the JAG, was given the authority to vacate or set aside findings and sentence in whole or in part, or to order a rehearing of such action as may seem appropriate in the circumstances. These provisions were designed to minimize aberrational procedures and to insure that an accused was afforded an orderly quasi-judicial hearing.

Greater regard for the individual was mirrored in steps taken to reduce or eliminate ill-advised courts-martial. This was to be accomplished through the exercise of greater care in proceedings prior to trial. When charged with a minor offense, the accused was not to be placed in confinement except under unusual circumstances. Important pretrial rights included a thorough and impartial investigation of the charges encompassing inquiries as to the truth of the matter, the form of the charge, and the disposition recommended in the interest of justice and discipline. At such investigations, the accused was to be afforded full opportunity to cross-examine witnesses against him and to present anything he chose in his own behalf in defense or mitigation. Any charges forwarded after such investigation were to be accompanied by a statement of the substance of the testimony taken on both sides.

The right of speedy trial incorporated in earlier articles was retained. Article 70 instructed military authorities, upon placing one under arrest or in confinement, to take immediate steps to bring the accused person to trial or to release him. A specific stipulation provided that in time of peace no person, against his objection, was to be brought to trial before a general court-martial within five days subsequent to the placing of charges against him. This was designed to provide time for the accused and his counsel to study the charges and plan the nature of their defense.

The importance of these changes is not to be denied. But the army was not disabused of its view that discipline was a function of command. As a result, the fact that the 1920 Code permitted the same officer to accuse, draft and direct charges, appoint defense counsel from the officers of his command, choose the members of the court, review and alter their decisions, and change any sentence the court might hand down, presaged further effort at reform at the appropriate time. In accordance with our general expectations—that large numbers of citizen soldiers is the key factor promoting liberalization of military law in the United States—the "appropriate time" was during and after World War II. In the interim between the wars, the army was allowed to diminish in personnel and in budget. Moreover, the peacetime draft still lay in the future.

Nine

World War II involved something like eleven million men in the United States Army alone. Of this number, 80,000 were convicted by general courts-martial and many thousands more by special and summary courts.[75] Of course, most of these soldiers were drafted into military service and their large numbers guaranteed that their views would be of considerable interest to Congress, particularly upon returning to civilian life. For Congress was alert not only to the number of persons actually serving in the armed forces but also to the even larger number of relatives and friends who were subject to influence by the experiences reported by returning servicemen.

As in World War I, abuses were freely reported and complaints about the system of military justice abounded. One private, twenty-three years of age, was sentenced to death for disobeying a captain's command. This was later commuted to life imprisonment with General Dwight D. Eisenhower's approval.[76] Five American soldiers who refused to obey an order at Fort McClelland, Alabama, were sentenced to five to thirty years at hard labor.[77] In another instance, a second lieutenant was convicted by a court-martial and dismissed from the service after having charges served on him an hour and twenty minutes before trial.[78] A general court-martial which sat in the case had refused the defendant's plea for more time. This led President Truman to grant a full and unconditional pardon to the lieutenant upon the recommendation of the War Department.[79]

In 1943 President Franklin D. Roosevelt was called upon to review so many court-martial cases that he appointed Samuel I. Rosenman as special counsel to the president with responsibility of advising the president in this area.[80]

The army, under Secretary of War Robert P. Patterson, set up special clemency boards to review sentences of general court-martial prisoners by the thousands. In 1944 Patterson announced that the army would review 27,500 court-martial decisions handed down in the stress of war and adjust if necessary any harsh sentences uncovered.[81] Such measures during the war were temporary and expedient and did not diminish concern in Congress over the principles of the system that produced these anomalies. One congressman testified that he had "knowledge of the fact that when a court does not please the commanding officer in the sentence imposed, that it finds itself dismissed, a new court appointed, and frequently the officers are detailed on rather undesirable assignments as the result of their action on the court."[82] Another introduced a bill requiring the defense counsel to have the same rank as the attorney for the prosecution in court-martial cases on the grounds that he knew of cases "where I feel that an injustice was done to the defendant through his attorney because the attorney happened to be of lower rank than the attorney for the prosecution."[83]

According to Congressman Mendel Rivers of South Carolina, "Every Member of this House, during the war years, has been deluged with complaints of autocracy in the han-

75 U.S., Congress, House, *Congressional Record*, 80th Cong., 2d sess., 14 January 1948, p. 157.
76 *New York Times*, 20 June 1945, p. 3.
77 Ibid., 14 April 1944, p. 5.
78 Ibid., 21 April 1945, p. 15.
79 Ibid.
80 Ibid., 15 September 1943, p. 30.
81 Ibid., 17 November 1944, p. 19.
82 U.S., Congress, House, *Congressional Record*, 80th Cong., 2d sess., 14 January 1948, p. 167.
83 Ibid.

dling of these courts martial throughout the Armed Forces. Everybody has had complaints, and they were just complaints. . . . The American Legion, the avc, the Amvets, the vfw and the New York County Bar Association and every legal organization of any real influence in this Nation has been clamoring, along with the American people, for a change in the situation." And Congressman Paul J. Kilday of Texas, ultimately destined to be a member of the United States Court of Military Appeals, said that "Prior to the war when the Army was composed of professional soldiers, all of whom knew the rules under which they were living and working, they experienced practically no difficulty. The difficulty arose when millions of civilians went into uniform. . . . Of course, these new officers and enlisted men were not professional soldiers, and they were not as familiar with the rules of the game as their professional predecessors had been. Therefore, even before the termination of the war, there was a very distinct demand that something be done toward revising the administration of military justice."[84]

In more general terms, the major defects alleged were nonuniform punishments, abuses of command influence, discrimination between enlisted men and officers, the use of unqualified defense counsel, and inadequate appellate procedures.

In 1944 and 1945 the War Department sent Colonel Phillip McCook to various theaters of operations in order to study the system of military justice in the field. In 1946 a War Department Advisory Committee on Military Justice was appointed by the secretary of war with Arthur D. Vanderbilt, the eminent New Jersey jurist, selected as committee chairman.[85] The committee consisted of outstanding lawyers and federal jurists from eight states and the District of Columbia. After nine months of study and hearings in Washington, New York, Philadelphia, Baltimore, and other

84 Ibid., pp. 161, 163.
85 Ibid., p. 157.

leading cities and after hearing testimony by the secretary of war, the chief of staff, the judge advocate general, the undersecretary of war, the commander of army ground forces, and representatives of five veterans organizations, the War Department was prepared to support certain changes in the system. Other studies of the system were underway at the same time both within Congress and without. However, no meaningful action was taken until January 1948, when the Armed Services Committee of the House of Representatives reported a bill to amend the Articles of War and improve the system of military justice.

The Elston bill, as amended, was passed by the House in 1948.[86] The bill incorporated a number of important changes in the Articles of War. Although the army opposed the idea, enlisted men and warrant officers were authorized to sit on general and special courts. For the first time, a member of the judge advocate general's department or an officer who was a member of the federal bar or the bar of the highest court of a state and who had been certified by the judge advocate general was required to be appointed for all general courts-martial. This was designed to insure that at least one official present during the general court proceeding would be familiar with judicial processes on the civil side and would be in a position to advise against procedural abuse.

Under the old Articles of War, the president had authority to exempt certain classes from trial by special and summary courts—a power that had been used to exempt officers. The effect on commanding officers was a general reluctance to subject officers to trial and possible dismissal by a general court when comparatively minor offenses were involved. On the other hand, enlisted men were regularly tried and convicted by special and summary courts for similar offenses. To rectify this, the 1948 revision subjected officers to special courts-martial for noncapital offenses for the first time.

[86] 62 Stat. 627.

Other provisions assured process to compel witnesses to appear and testify, prohibited compulsory self-incrimination, and established a Board of Review and a Judicial Council in the judge advocate general's department. Each of these bodies was to be composed of three general officers of the judge advocate general's department. Additional boards and councils were to be appointed if needed. With the approval of the judge advocate general, the Board of Review was empowered to modify or vacate findings and sentences under certain conditions. Such changes were to be confirmed by the Judicial Council. The council was also empowered to confirm or rule upon cases in which the Board of Review wished to make modifications and the judge advocate general did not agree.

Boards of review in the armed services date from a War Department order in 1918 which required consideration by a Board of Review in the office of the judge advocate general or in a branch office before the implementation of serious sentences by courts-martial. This order resulted from an instance in Houston, Texas, early in World War I in which certain soldiers who had mutinied were executed the day after being sentenced to death. The War Department order was put in statutory form in the 1920 Revision of the Articles of War and was modified further in the 1948 Revision.

In order to reduce command control, the 1948 legislation established a separate judge advocate general's corps with a separate promotion list. This was opposed vigorously by the Department of the Army on the ground that discipline would be affected.[87] The general congressional response to this was essentially that at some point justice is paramount to discipline.

Significant advances were made in regard to defense counsel. By the new legislation, the authority convening a special or general court was required to appoint a trial

[87] U.S., Congress, House, *Congressional Record*, 80th Cong., 2d sess., 14 January 1948, p. 157.

judge advocate and a defense counsel and one or more assistant trial judge advocates and assistant defense counsel when necessary. If available, these persons were to be members of the judge advocate general's department or officers who were members of the bar of a federal court or of the highest court of the state. While the loophole, if available, permitted the appointment of nonlawyers as defense counsel, it was stipulated that in all cases in which the officer appointed as trial judge advocate was a member of the judge advocate general's department or a member of the federal bar or the bar of the highest state court, the defense counsel must have the same qualifications. Moreover, persons who acted as a member, a trial judge advocate, an assistant trial judge advocate, or an investigating officer in any case were barred from serving as a defense counsel or assistant defense counsel unless expressly requested to do so by the accused. Similarly, defense personnel were not permitted to serve subsequently as a member of the prosecution and no person who had served in either prosecutorial or defense capacity was to be permitted to act as a staff judge advocate to the reviewing or confirming authority upon the same case.

In an entirely new article, the military defendant to be tried by a general court was permitted upon his request to be represented at all pretrial investigations by counsel of his own selection, civil or military, if reasonably available, otherwise by counsel to be appointed by the officer exercising general courts-martial jurisdiction over the command. This article not only assured the right to a pretrial investigation of the charges, the validity of the charges, and the disposition of the case but also guaranteed the right of cross-examination and the right of the defendant to present witnesses or anything else he may care to offer in his behalf.

Upon passage, the Elston bill was sent to the Senate where it was directed to the Armed Services Committee. The committee under the chairmanship of Senator Chance

Gurney "sat" on the bill for four months and seemed to be making no progress toward reporting it. The reluctance of the committee to report the bill was related directly to the opposition of the War Department to a separate judge advocate general's department with a separate promotion list and the authority to remit, reduce, or suspend sentences. As a consequence of this inaction, Senator James P. Kem of Missouri introduced the House bill in verbatim form, as an amendment to the Selective Service Act of 1948, then under consideration on the floor of the Senate. The Selective Service Act of 1948 with the Kem amendment passed by a vote of 44 to 39.[88] The amendment contained forty-nine articles and covered six pages of fine print in the *Congressional Record* and passed in spite of appeals from the Armed Services Committee chairman and others that the committee be permitted to complete its consideration of the bill. This testifies to the strength of feeling in the Senate concerning the desirability of this reform and reflects the pressures which many senators were receiving from their constituents to act promptly on the matter.

In arguing that the Senate committee should be allowed to complete its review of the House bill, Senator Gurney stressed that the Elston bill referred only to the army whereas the reforms proposed therein could be applied to the entire national military establishment. In fact, Gurney revealed correspondence with Secretary of War James Forrestal concerning the desirability of a code of military justice to cover all the services. Forrestal, for his part, agreed on May 14, 1948, to appoint a committee to study the matter. The committee, subsequently appointed, consisted of Professor Edmund M. Morgan, Jr., of the Harvard Law School as chairman, Undersecretary of the Navy John Kenney, Assistant Secretary of the Army Gordon Gray, Assistant Secretary of the Air Force Eugene M. Zuckert,

88 U.S., Congress, House, *Congressional Record*, 80th Cong., 2d sess., 9 June 1948, p. 7516.

and Felix E. Larkin, the assistant general counsel of the Department of Defense.[89]

The Supreme Court was relatively, if not absolutely, inactive regarding right to counsel until 1938 insofar as the federal courts were concerned. But in 1932 the landmark case of *Powell* v. *Alabama*[90] carried heavy implications for the principle in state courts. Since the Bill of Rights does not apply to the states, it has been necessary to develop its application through the due-process and equal-protection clauses of the Fourteenth Amendment, which is applicable to the states. While this has been done in a piecemeal fashion, the cumulative effect has been substantial.

In the *Powell* case, seven Negro boys allegedly raped two white girls in a freight car near Scottsboro, Alabama. The Negroes were brought to trial without counsel being provided until the trial was about to commence—this in spite of the fact that the defendants were "young, ignorant, illiterate, [and] surrounded by hostile sentiment."[91] The state's highest court found no violation of the state constitution in this arrangement, but the Supreme Court ruled that the Alabama court had failed to provide "reasonable time and opportunity to secure counsel."[92] In the circumstances, the Supreme Court thought this a violation of constitutional due process. In explaining its rule, the Court delineated its view that assignment of counsel is necessary under due process given a capital offense, inability of the defendant to employ counsel, and the inability of the defendant to defend himself because of ignorance, feeblemindedness, illiteracy, etc.

Read literally, the rule of the *Powell* case leaves unanswered a major question: Does the presence of one or two of these factors bring the rule into operation and if so which ones? This matter has been clarified by subsequent court

[89] Ibid., p. 7520.
[90] 287 U.S. 45.
[91] Ibid., p. 57.
[92] Ibid., p. 71.

decisions finding a violation of due process in all capital cases in which effective counsel has not been provided. Thus for ten years, the rule was absolute that capital cases required effective counsel in state courts. The constitutional requirement in noncapital cases was left unanswered during the decade.

On the federal side, the decision of the Supreme Court in *Johnson* v. *Zerbst*[93] changed the longstanding rule that federal courts were under no obligation to appoint counsel for those unable to obtain them in noncapital cases. The federal crimes act of 1790 required court-appointed counsel in capital cases, leaving the implication that furnished the basis for the rule in noncapital cases. In *Johnson,* a counterfeiting prosecution, the court noted that due process requires a hearing but added a new thought—that, by definition, the hearing must be meaningful and that right to counsel was necessary to make it so. Thus in all criminal prosecutions, federal courts were obliged to provide counsel if unobtainable otherwise.

Though this rule permits the possibility of waiver, circumstances determine whether the waiver will be approved by appellate authority. This uncertainty makes the waiver route a hazardous one for prosecutors who wish to have their convictions upheld and undoubtedly has discouraged reliance on the doctrine.

The *Johnson* rule was subsequently incorporated into the federal rules of criminal procedure by a rule stating that "If the defendant appears in court without counsel, the court shall advise him of his right to counsel and assign counsel to represent him at every stage of the proceeding unless he elects to proceed without counsel or is able to obtain counsel."[94] The "Johnson Right," therefore, arises at arraignment where the defendant is obliged to plead to the indictment.

Four years after *Johnson* v. *Zerbst,* the Supreme Court

[93] 304 U.S. 458.
[94] Rule 44, F.C.A. Rules, p. 137.

was presented with a state case pressing the implications of the new federal rule in state jurisdictions. Unlike *Powell, Betts* v. *Brady*[95] was a noncapital case—a burglary in Maryland for which Smith Betts was tried and convicted without a jury. After the court refused to appoint counsel, Betts defended himself unsuccessfully, refraining at the time from waiving his claimed privilege to have counsel appointed. Using a "fair trial" rule, the Maryland Court of Appeals affirmed Betts's conviction and denied his claim that due process had been violated. The Supreme Court adopted the fair trial rule, Justice Owen Roberts' opinion for the Court, denying that the Fourteenth Amendment incorporated the Sixth Amendment as such. The opinion went on to stress that the denial of due process depended on the "totality of facts in a given case." In *Betts,* the opinion concluded, the defendant had received a fair trial in spite of the absence of counsel and in the circumstances Betts was not deprived of any constitutionally protected privileges. This, then, was the status of constitutional law in the right to counsel area on the major questions that had been brought before the Supreme Court up to 1948, the date of the passage of the Elston Act.

It may be useful at this point to summarize the enactments of Congress and Court on right to counsel in military and civil courts from the birth of the Republic to 1950. All civil courts in this country have recognized the right of criminal defendants to provide their own counsel throughout the history of the nation. This was not a right traditionally recognized before military tribunals. It was contrary to English Common Law at the establishment of the nation, but it was consistent with developments after 1836. Federal legislation of 1790 granted the right to appointed counsel in federal courts in capital cases but not in noncapital cases. On the military side, this was not quite matched by the 1806 provision that the judge advocate (or military prosecutor) prevent leading questions to witnesses

95 316 U.S. 455.

and protect military defendants against self-incrimination.

By the time that the federal protection of 1790 had been extended to noncapital cases, military law had made several advances, none of which occurred until 1916. In that year the military defendant gained the statutory right to counsel of his own selection in general and special courts, where such counsel was reasonably available. In 1920 Congress required, for the first time, the appointment of a defense counsel in each general or special court-martial. At the same time the accused was explicitly granted the freedom to employ civilian counsel and, if available, the defendant could choose the military counsel to be appointed.

In 1948 the new Articles specified that the appointed counsel was to be a member of the judge advocate general's department or a member of the bar of a federal court or the highest court for a state. And if the trial judge advocate was a lawyer, the convening authority was required to appoint a lawyer as defense counsel. These rights were also extended to pretrial investigations in slightly diluted form.

This brief summary pinpoints the fact that the accused military defendant gained more in this area in the thirty-five years between 1915 and 1950 than in the one hundred twenty-five years between 1790 and 1915. These later gains stemmed, on the whole, not from a liberalization of army philosophy regarding military law and procedure but from the dissatisfaction of large numbers of conscripted citizens during World Wars I and II, our system of government which enables the effective communication of grievances to legislators by those to whom the legislators are responsible, and the vigorous leadership provided by a few enlightened reformers who added intellectual and theoretical dimensions to the movement.

Ten

The Morgan Committee appointed by Secretary Forrestal in 1949 ultimately produced the Uniform Code of Military Justice (UCMJ). The military services have operated under the code, as amended by the Military Justice Act of 1968 (MJA), since 1951.[96] The effect of the enactment was to nullify the Articles of War and the governing codes of the navy and air force. The UCMJ, then, is the constitutional law of the armed forces. Manuals of courts-martial are promulgated by the president and have the force of law but must be, in content, pursuant to the UCMJ.

Although the code retains many of the revisions of the Elston Act regarding the jurisdiction of general, special, and summary courts as to persons, offenses, and punishments, its provisions on individual rights go somewhat beyond anything enacted earlier. The code, in readily understandable form, provides new emphasis on fair trial procedures and on eliminating undue command control. It requires that charges and specifications be signed under oath and that suspects be warned of their right to remain silent. Authority for pretrial arrest and confinement is limited, while undue haste in the trial of a military defendant is prohibited. Provisions are inserted to protect the independence of the court-martial and to guarantee the military defendant the right to enlisted men on the court which tries him. Specific provisions assure protection against double jeopardy and cruel and unusual punishment. As in the civil courts, the presumption of innocence is adopted and the burden of proving guilt is on the prosecutor.

In the system established by the UCMJ, as in the state and federal legal systems, the criminal process follows three stages: the pretrial investigation, the trial, and appellate proceedings. Under Article 32 of the UCMJ, the accused may not be prosecuted by a general court until a thorough and objective investigation of the charge has occurred. As in civilian life, the military defendant has the right to counsel at this stage. Since the pretrial investigation incorporates the right of the defense to call and cross-examine witnesses, the proceedings constitute an important source of discovery. The significance of counsel at this stage lies in the fact that the evidence developed by the defense counsel may determine whether the convening authority prefers charges in a formal trial setting.

The military defendant at the pretrial investigation may select his own civilian counsel, select military counsel, or have counsel appointed for him. With the first option, the defendant must pay the legal fees and must select counsel who is a member of the bar of a federal court, the bar of a foreign country, or the bar of the highest court of a state. His selection of specific military counsel is limited by the reasonable availability of the person selected.

These same general privileges are required for a general court-martial. A trial counsel or prosecutor must be detailed who is a law school graduate or a licensed attorney certified by the judge advocate general. He prosecutes in the name of the United States and prepares the record. He may be assisted by additional counsel if necessary. If a defense counsel is assigned, he must have the same qualifications as the prosecutor in order to assure the defendant every opportunity of creating a reasonable doubt about his guilt. This salutory principle has not yet been incorporated into trial procedures in nonmilitary courts. It is also unnecessary for the defendant to request the assignment of counsel. If he is without such help, it must be provided.

In the special court-martial, the defendant must have

96 64 Stat. 108; 82 Stat. 1335, effective Aug. 24, 1969.

counsel. But while neither trial nor defense counsel are required to be lawyers, the MJA encourages it. In line with the equalizing principle, if trial counsel is an attorney the defense counsel must also be a qualified lawyer. The accused, of course, may employ qualified civilian counsel or have additional military counsel on request where available.

Before the summary court, counsel are not required. Indeed, the summary court officer investigates the charges, acts as judge and jury, and as trial or defense counsel. The loss of the greater protection afforded for general and special courts is compensated for in part by allowing the defendant to call and cross-examine witnesses and to introduce evidence in his own behalf.

The distinction between the right to counsel afforded the accused in these three courts correlates with the risk the defendant runs at each level. The general court may impose any authorized penalty up to and including the death sentence and can try any person subject to the code for any offense punishable under it. The special court, on the other hand, can try any person subject to the code for noncapital offenses (and for capital offenses under presidential regulations). It can levy any punishment not forbidden by the code with the exception of death, forfeiture of six months pay in excess of two-thirds, confinement at hard labor for periods in excess of three months, incarceration beyond six months duration, dismissal of an officer, or dishonorable discharge. The lesser jurisdiction and punitive power of the special court may account for the lesser protection afforded the accused. As a justification, this seems to be a departure from the jurisprudential principle that the function of counsel is to minimize the chances that an innocent person will be convicted or to assure or require the prosecutor to establish the guilt of the accused beyond a reasonable doubt. The severity of the penalty that may be levied or the breadth of the jurisdiction is not germane to this principle, although some courts have reflected the consideration in its holdings.

In the summary court, where the right to counsel is non-existent, jurisdiction and punitive power are most limited. This court can try any person subject to the code for non-capital offenses only, but officers, warrant officers, cadets or midshipmen are excepted. It can reduce the grade of an enlisted man, confine him for up to a month, restrict him for up to two months, and impose fines equal to two-thirds of one month's salary. An alleviation of the absence of counsel at this stage is provided in Article 20, which gives an accused the right to object to a summary court-martial. In that event, such a person may be tried by a special or general court. However, the conditions under which one might object to summary trial may occur infrequently, for the convening authority has the discretion of offering trial for a lesser charge before a summary court or trial on a more serious charge before a general or special court. Since the defendant tried by these courts runs greater risk if found guilty, he may not desire to exercise the option.

Subsequent to trial, all cases are reviewed in the office of the judge advocate general, and if legal error is discovered or if the judge advocate general thinks it desirable, the record will be sent to a Court of Military Review. If the case comes from a general court or a special court involving a bad conduct discharge or affects a general or flag officer, a death sentence, dishonorable discharge, or the discharge of an officer, or confinement for a year or more, the judge advocate general must refer the matter to such a court. These courts are composed of lawyers and may be composed of both civilian and military personnel. A Court of Military Review has the authority to dismiss charges and thus it is vital for a convicted defendant to have adequate representation at this stage of the proceedings. Article 70 requires that the defendant be represented before the court by military appellate defense counsel if he requests or in any event if the United States has counsel. He also retains the privilege of employing civilian counsel.

Appeal from the action of a Court of Military Review lies

to the United States Court of Military Appeals (USCMA), established by the Uniform Code of Military Justice (UCMJ). This court consists of three civilian judges appointed by the president for fifteen-year terms—one of whom is designated by the president as chief judge. Administratively, the court is situated in the Department of Defense, but its operations are as independent as those of any other federal court. The code requires the Court of Military Appeals to review all cases in which the death sentence has been approved by a Court of Military Review or in which a general or flag officer has been sentenced. In addition, it takes all other cases forwarded by the judge advocate general after action by the appropriate Court of Military Review and may accept, at its discretion, other cases on petition of the accused. The right of the accused here does not extend to those general court-martial cases which the judge advocate general may forward at his discretion.

On an appeal to the USCMA, the accused is entitled to civilian counsel if provided by him. Appellate defense counsel is assigned to represent the interest of the accused and, if civilian counsel is employed, serves as assistant defense counsel if the defendant so desires. Before the court, oral argument is required in all cases unless waived by the court itself. Each party is normally allowed thirty minutes for argument.

The Uniform Code of Military Justice was adopted as a result of various inadequacies identified in the military legal system during the two world wars. But when President Truman signed the measure on May 6, 1950, he remarked that "the code, good as it is, does not go far enough in its changes. In one important respect, especially, it falls short. It retains the command control of the court-martial. The court is actually appointed and convened by a commanding officer of the individual to be tried. This necessarily leaves the system open to the charge of the possible presence of prejudice or pressure from time to time."[97]

97 *New York Times*, 8 May 1950, p. 22.

Traditionally the commanding officer has been empowered to order trial for an accused, select the members of the court, appoint both prosecution and defense counsel, and review the court's findings and its sentence. President Truman's remark was occasioned by the fact that the new code divested the commanding officer of none of these powers. In hearings on the new code in 1949, Morgan testified that these powers were left because of the military nature of courts-martial.[98] If this were recognized as a significant distinction, some of the criticisms of the system of military justice might be weakened. However, it has not been easy for some students of military justice to accept the fact that the men chosen to serve as counsel, judge, and jury are directly responsible to the convening authority for assignment, promotion, and efficiency evaluation. One writer has suggested that command control could be divested by giving the judge advocate general the right to appoint general and special courts-martial, defense counsel, and the authority to review the action of the courts.[99] The code itself gives some recognition to the problem in Article 37 which forbids command interference with court-martial proceedings. But procedures for protecting the accused from such interference are not effectively established.

In regard to counsel, the new code incorporated some highly significant changes. Apart from the Articles of War and other statutory commands and prohibitions, the defense forces have always had the discretion to issue rules and regulations and operating procedures for courts-martial so long as such orders do not conflict with statutory or constitutional provisions. In 1861 a military writer noted that lawyers were apt to be very forward and troublesome persons and consequently that courts-martial "wisely . . . exer-

[98] F. R. Dixon and Rudolph S. Zadrik, "Military Justice—A Uniform Code for the Armed Services," *Western Reserve Law Review* 2 (Dec. 1950): 147-61; U.S., Congress, *House, Hearings before Subcommittee of the Committee on Armed Services on S857 and HR 4080,* 81st Cong., 1st sess., 1949, p. 76.

[99] Dixon and Zadrik, "Military Justice," p. 149.

cised the right of refusing their assent for the appearance of such persons."[100] In 1875 another writer noted no relaxation in courts-martial "as to the silence of professional advisors and their taking no part in the proceedings."[101] But in 1865 navy regulations permitted the assignment of counsel in the form of a commissioned, warrant, or petty officer if requested by the accused. If so assigned, counsel could appear on behalf of the accused and cross-examine witnesses, but he was not allowed to present a written defense nor was he allowed any protracted oral defense. In 1890 the army issued a regulation requiring the appointment of a suitable officer in general courts-martial to represent the accused if requested. However, it was not until 1948 that lawyer-counsel was required, and this requirement was restricted to general courts only.

The UCMJ requires the appointment of trial and defense counsel, both of whom must be lawyers and who must be certified as qualified by the judge advocate general of the appropriate branch of service. These requirements are new to military justice and obviously constitute a continuing liberalization of court-martial procedures toward greater protection for the individual. In special courts-martial, however, the code effected no change. Thus, while we can say that in general courts the military defendant has rights comparable to those of a criminal defendant in a federal court, the same statement cannot be made for special courts. Article 27 of the code provides that if trial counsel in the special court is qualified to act before a general court, then the defense counsel must be similarly qualified. Likewise, if the trial counsel is a judge advocate or Military Judge, or a member of the bar of a federal court or a highest state court, so must be the defense counsel. But trial counsel are not required absolutely to have these qualifications—an omission which has rather direct consequences for military

100 Ziegel W. Neff, "Right to Counsel in Special Courts-Martial," *Judge Advocate Journal* (Oct. 1962): 58-68.
101 Ibid.

defendants. In the navy and Marine Corps where qualified counsel may be in short supply, the convening authority may appoint nonlawyer trial counsel, thereby reducing the legal skills to which the military defendant is entitled for his defense. While it may be suggested that two ill-trained advocates introduce some kind of equality between the competing parties, the rights of an individual are at stake and the individual may have more to lose through inadequate representation than the prosecuting authority. The question is now being raised as to whether or not the federal Constitution requires that an accused defendant before a special court-martial be furnished lawyer-counsel. Since the Sixth Amendment is ambiguous on this point, the matter can be argued either way. The MJA provides that if a lawyer-counsel is not appointed, the convening authority must append an explanation to the record. But this is hardly the kind of guarantee needed.

Other critics of the code have suggested that lawyer-counsel should not be required in all courts-martial. They point to the large number of trials, the shortage of lawyers and the delay caused by such shortage, the presence of a trained and experienced Military Judge on the courts, and the fact that many of the issues controverted are quite simple from a legal point of view and consequently need no trained attorney to unravel them. While it is indeed true that courts-martial occur in fairly large numbers, it is difficult to see how such a fact justifies an inadequate defense in any particular case. There has traditionally been a consistent shortage of lawyers, but this could probably be alleviated by assigning those in the service who are not engaged in legal work to the judge advocate general's office in larger numbers as well as making service in the judge advocate's corps more attractive to those law school graduates not currently in the services. As to the simplicity of many of the issues, this argument overlooks the complexity of procedures required to see that justice is done in military courts. Counsel is needed to determine what plea to make, to conduct the trial, to focus consideration of the court on those matters that should be influential in the fixing of a sentence, and to determine whether an appeal should be taken. Regardless of how simple the issue at trial may be, it is difficult to see how the presence of a trained attorney would fail to add substantially greater protection for individual rights.

The year 1951 marks the end of significant congressional change in military law. In the period 1951-1968, the development of military law has occurred primarily in the USCMA through the decisions made in the cases that have come before it. With the establishment of the court, it is no longer necessary to wait for Congress to provide innovations designed to improve the system of military justice. This is not to imply that Congress has lost all interest in the matter. Indeed, a number of bills designed to improve the system have been introduced in the Congress during this seventeen-year period. However, like the Supreme Court, the United States Court of Military Appeals is involved in the interpretation of a "Constitution" which may grow —in which the guaranteed rights for criminal defendants in military trials may expand in the same way that such rights in the federal Constitution have been enlarged. It will be instructive to examine the treatment of right to counsel in the USCMA in order to compare any doctrinal and substantive developments that may have occurred with similar developments on the civilian side.

Eleven

Prior to 1960 the Bill of Rights in the federal Constitution was applicable to the federal government but not to the states. The First Amendment may be considered an exception to this general statement, since provisions of that Amendment had been incorporated in the due-process clause of the Fourteenth Amendment. The search and seizure provisión of the Fourth Amendment is also a possible exception, since the Court held in 1949 that the security of one's privacy against arbitrary intrusion by the police was implicit in the concept of ordered liberty and as such enforceable against the states through the due-process clause. This holding was diluted somewhat by the refusal of the Court to require state courts to exclude evidence obtained by state officers through unreasonable searches and seizures. Some students of the Court interpreted *Powell* v. *Alabama* as incorporating the right to counsel into the due-process clause of the Fourteenth Amendment. *Betts* v. *Brady,* however, emphasized that no such incorporation had taken place. The rule stated there is that right to counsel is required where its denial would be shocking to a universal sense of justice. Whether such a criterion is met was said to be a function of the total circumstances in which the denial occurred.

When the occasion demands, the Court has emphasized that a defendant in a state criminal trial has an unqualified right to be heard through his own counsel.[102] This point, however, has not been significantly contended. The more important question concerns the obligation of states to furnish counsel in various state proceedings. Subsequent to

Betts v. *Brady,* a large number of state counsel cases continued to come to the Court. In many of these cases, violation of due process was found in the refusal of the state to furnish counsel. However, these holdings turned on total factual circumstances, although particular factors received emphasis in one case or another. Thus, whether the offense was a capital one, whether the conduct of the trial judge was questionable, the youth or ignorance of the defendant or the complexity of legal issues were factors present in cases decided for the defendant.

The determination of decisions through total factual circumstances has led to some anomalous results. In 1931 a nineteen-year-old robber was sentenced to serve from fifteen to thirty years in a New York state prison. After serving fourteen years of this sentence he petitioned the New York Court asking that his sentence be vacated and set aside on the grounds that at the time of his arraignment, guilty plea, and sentence, he was unfamiliar with legal proceedings and not represented by counsel. The court had neither asked whether he desired counsel nor advised him of his right to counsel. Under these conditions, he argued, his guilty plea should not have been accepted and the acceptance of it deprived him of his liberty without due process of law. Investigation of this charge revealed that the petitioner was without counsel when he was arraigned and when he pleaded guilty and that the court failed to inform him of his right to counsel. However, it was shown that counsel was provided on the day of sentencing and participated in long hearings on that day. In this situation, the Supreme Court decided that the defendant's right to counsel had been observed, suggesting that if error had occurred prior to assignment of counsel, there remained ample opportunity to correct earlier errors at the hearing.[103] Justice Frank Murphy dissenting described the situation revealed by the record in this case as a "complete travesty of justice."

In a California case, the petitioner under sentence of

[102] *Chandler* v. *Fretag,* 348 U.S. 3; *In re Groban,* 352 U.S. 334.
[103] *Canizio* v. *New York,* 327 U.S. 82.

death for the murder of his paramour claimed that his conviction in a California court contravened his rights under the Fourteenth Amendment. His confession was allegedly coerced and if not, he charged, it occurred while he was without counsel. The Supreme Court recognized that the defendant had been denied his request to employ an attorney and that the Fourteenth Amendment prohibited the use of coerced confessions in state prosecutions. But since the defendant was a college graduate with some law school training—a person who knew of his right to keep silent—no constitutional violation was found. The confession occurred in a context in which the police informed the defendant of his right to refuse to answer questions, gave him coffee, milk, and a sandwich, and allowed him to smoke whenever he liked. In these circumstances the Court thought that absence of counsel was of no constitutional significance.[104]

This case raised the issue of right to counsel in the custodial period prior to trial and led four justices on the Supreme Court to assert, in dissent, that the due-process clause requires that the accused who wants counsel should have one at any time after the moment of arrest. In a case decided a year earlier, the Court had held that a witness before a grand jury or other investigatory body cannot insist, as a matter of federal constitutional right, to be represented by counsel. The same four justices dissented finding it unconstitutional for a state to compel a person to appear alone before any law enforcement officer and give testimony in secret against his will. The question of the 1960s, then, has been the point at which due process requires that criminal defendants be furnished counsel in state proceedings. Given the appointment of one more justice with an outlook similar to that expressed by the four dissenters in *Crooker,* future doctrinal development in this area could be safely predicted.

Arthur J. Goldberg took his seat on the Supreme Court

[104] *Crooker* v. *California,* 357 U.S. 433.

in October 1962. Two years later, the Court decided the case of *Escobedo* v. *Illinois*.[105] The four dissenters from *Crooker* joined an opinion written by Goldberg with Justices John Marshall Harlan, Byron White, Tom Clark, and Potter Stewart dissenting. *Escobedo* is a landmark case which we shall consider momentarily. But first, we should consider three earlier cases decided in the 1960s. The first of these is *Hamilton* v. *Alabama*,[106] decided in 1961. This was a capital case with petitioner being sentenced to death on an indictment charging breaking and entering a dwelling at night with intent to ravish. On appeal, Hamilton claimed he had been denied counsel at the time of arraignment in violation of the Fourteenth Amendment. The Supreme Court declined to hold, in an opinion by Justice William Douglas, that the Constitution requires counsel at arraignment in every case. However, it affirmed that arraignment is so critical a stage of Alabama criminal procedure that denial of counsel at arraignment required reversal of the conviction. This decision was reached in spite of the fact that no prejudice to the defendant was shown.

In *White* v. *Maryland*,[107] decided in 1963, the Supreme Court was faced with a denial of counsel at the preliminary hearing stage of a Maryland proceeding. A guilty plea made by a criminal defendant at that point became a permanent part of the record and was introduced at trial even though the plea had been changed subsequently. The Court held that the preliminary hearing stage in Maryland procedure was just as critical as the arraignment stage in Alabama proceedings, since a lack of procedural knowledge in either case could cost the defendant his life or liberty. Consequently it found a violation of due process.

Finally, in the same year, the Supreme Court was presented the opportunity of reevaluating its holding in *Betts*

105 378 U.S. 478.
106 368 U.S. 52.
107 373 U.S. 59.

v. *Brady.* That opportunity occurred in the case of *Gideon* v. *Wainwright,*[108] a case which has gained considerable notoriety. *Gideon* was a Florida case in which the petitioner was charged with having broken into a poolroom with intent to commit a misdemeanor. At trial, Gideon appeared wihout counsel and asked the Florida court to appoint one for him. He was told in reply that the court could appoint counsel to represent a defendant only when that person was charged with a capital offense and that the laws of Florida did not permit the appointment of counsel otherwise. As a consequence of this refusal, Gideon conducted his own defense, was found guilty, and sentenced to serve five years in the state penitentiary. The Supreme Court granted certiorari, appointed counsel for Gideon, and requested both sides to discuss the question "Should this Court's holding in *Betts v. Brady* be reconsidered?"[109]

The similarity of the facts in *Gideon* and *Betts* is striking. Both involved a robbery charge; both men requested counsel and were refused on essentially the same grounds; both served as their own counsel during the trials; and both were convicted and sentenced to prison terms. Since the Court's holding in *Betts* refused to extend the Sixth Amendment's right to counsel provision against the states, a reconsideration of that case raised the question anew.

In an opinion by Justice Hugo Black, the Court noted that a number of provisions in the Bill of Rights had been incorporated into the Fourteenth Amendment, thereby making such rights obligatory on the states. Specifically mentioned were freedoms of speech, press, religion, assembly, association, and petition for redress of grievances; the Fifth Amendment's command that private property shall not be taken for public use without just compensation; the prohibition against unreasonable searches and seizures in the Fourth Amendment; and the ban against cruel and unusual punishment in the Eighth Amendment. Incorporation in

108 372 U.S. 335.
109 Ibid., p. 338.

each case was said to depend on the requirements of ordered liberty and, in case of trial rights, on what is "fundamental and essential to a fair trial."

Accepting the assumption in *Betts* v. *Brady* that such "fundamental" provisions of the Bill of Rights are made obligatory upon the states by the Fourteenth Amendment, the Court in *Gideon* reversed the finding in *Betts* that "appointment of counsel is not a fundamental right, essential to a fair trial."[110] Black's argument, essentially, was that "lawyers in criminal courts are necessities, not luxuries."[111] Since governments, both state and federal, spend large sums of money to try criminal defendants, the least that the state can do is to see that the defendant has the assistance of one who is familiar with such matters as the rules of evidence, the propriety of the charge, and the competence to judge whether an indictment is good or bad. Three justices concurred in this opinion; no dissenting votes were cast.

While the holding in *Gideon* constituted a major change in the constitutional law governing right to counsel, it left open a number of questions. In general, *Gideon* stands for the proposition that in criminal prosecutions, state courts must furnish counsel to a defendant upon request. However, since the Florida crime was a felony, *Gideon* leaves open the question of whether the right to counsel attaches to misdemeanors. *Gideon* may also be said to hold that the right to counsel attaches at the critical stage of criminal proceedings which in general have been defined as arraignment. Whether the rule of the case is retroactive is not answered by the Black opinion. In relying upon *Gideon* as a precedent, a vast majority of lower courts has subsequently held that counsel attaches only to felonies and that the rule is retroactive.

Escobedo v. *Illinois* picks up the line of doctrinal development indicated by the *Gideon* holding and extends the right of counsel in state criminal prosecutions to the prear-

110 Ibid., p. 340.
111 Ibid., p. 344.

raignment stage. Escobedo was a twenty-two year old of Mexican extraction with no record of previous experience with the police. On the night of January 19, 1960, Escobedo's brother-in-law was fatally shot. At 2:30 A.M. the next morning, Escobedo was arrested without a warrant and interrogated. After refusing to make a statement, he was released at 5:00 P.M. on the same day pursuant to a state court writ of habeas corpus. On the evening of January 30, Escobedo was rearrested, handcuffed, and informed by the police that they had the necessary evidence and that he, Escobedo, might as well admit to the crime. At this time Escobedo was in a police car en route to the police station, but he requested the opportunity to speak with his lawyer. The lawyer was refused his request to see Escobedo at the police station on the ground that police questioning had not been concluded. At this point no charge had been formally made, but Escobedo was in custody and could not leave of his own free will. In spite of repeated requests by both the attorney and Escobedo, no contact with counsel was permitted until Escobedo had made incriminating statements to the police. It was conceded by the police that no one advised Escobedo of his constitutional rights during the course of the interrogation. Subsequently Escobedo moved to suppress the incriminating statement, but the motions were denied; he was convicted of murder and appealed the conviction to the Supreme Court of Illinois. Ultimately that court affirmed the conviction and the United States Supreme Court granted certiorari.

The key question for the Supreme Court was whether to extend the Sixth Amendment right of counsel to the interrogation stage of a criminal prosecution. In an opinion by Justice Goldberg, the Court pointed out that when Escobedo requested, and was denied, an opportunity to consult with his lawyer, the investigation had ceased to be a general investigation of an unsolved crime. At that point Escobedo had become the accused and the purpose of the interrogation was to secure a confession of guilt notwithstanding

Escobedo's constitutional right not to confess. Observing that the right to use counsel at the formal trial would be a very hollow thing if, for all practical purposes, the conviction was already assured by pretrial examination, the Goldberg opinion went on to state that where "the investigation is no longer a general inquiry into an unsolved crime but has begun to focus on a particular suspect, the suspect has been taken into police custody, the police carry out a process of interrogation that lends itself to eliciting incriminating statements, the suspect has requested and been denied an opportunity to consult with his lawyer, and the police have not effectively warned him of his absolute constitutional right to remain silent, the accused has been denied the assistance of counsel in violation of the Sixth Amendment to the Constitution . . . and that no statement elicited by the police during the interrogation may be used against him at a criminal trial."

As the dissenters pointed out, the effect of this decision was to move the point at which an accused is entitled to counsel back to the time when the prosecution begins to focus on him. Although the lengthy statement of the holding above suggests that it is limited to the facts of the case, it may be expected that, given the continuation of current trends, the rule will become more general in its application. It may also be noted that the *Escobedo* ruling, in effect, abandons the voluntary-involuntary tests for admissibility of confessions. Under *Escobedo* it makes no difference whether the confession is voluntary; if it is made without benefit of counsel during the interrogation stage, or subsequently, it is suspect as evidence and very likely inadmissible at the formal trial stage. The *Escobedo* holding also encroaches upon the self-incrimination provision of the Fifth Amendment and, in effect, deprives one of the right to incriminate himself in the event counsel is not present as a witness. Whether one is compelled to issue incriminating statements is no longer the question. Indeed, the *Escobedo* holding moved the Court closer to the proposition that nothing said by one accused of crime subsequent to arrest may be used against him in a formal criminal trial.

The case of *Miranda* v. *Arizona*,[112] decided in 1966, dealt primarily with protection against self-incrimination. However, certain aspects of the Court's opinion touched significantly on right to counsel. In March 1963 Ernesto Miranda was arrested at his home and taken to a police station in Phoenix. There he was identified by a complaining witness and taken to an interrogation room where he was questioned by two police officers. Two hours later the officers produced a written confession signed by Miranda. At trial, the written statement was admitted into evidence, Miranda was found guilty of kidnapping and rape, and was sentenced to twenty to thirty years in prison on each count. The Arizona Supreme Court found no defects in the conviction, and certiorari was granted by the United States Supreme Court where a reversal of the conviction was obtained.

In reaching its decision, the Arizona Supreme Court emphasized the fact that Miranda had not specifically requested counsel and it was stipulated by the prosecution that during his interrogation, Miranda was not advised that he had a right to have an attorney present under the holding in *Escobedo*. On review, the Supreme Court, in an opinion by Chief Justice Earl Warren, held that statements obtained during incommunicado interrogation in a police station without full warning of constitutional rights violate the Fifth Amendment privilege against self-incrimination. The opinion went on to say that although the defendant may waive his right to counsel and his right to remain silent, there can be no questioning at any stage of the interrogation process if the defendant indicates a desire to consult with his attorney before speaking. If the defendant has no attorney or cannot afford to employ one, he must be advised of his right to have one appointed. Warren stressed that informing the defendant of his right to consult a lawyer

[112] 384 U.S. 474.

or to have an attorney present during an interrogation is an absolute prerequisite to interrogation. The Fifth and Sixth Amendments were integrated through the proposition that an individual held for interrogation must be clearly informed of his right to consult a lawyer and to have a lawyer with him during interrogation in order to protect the Fifth Amendment privilege.

It would be too much to say that the right to counsel exists, subsequent to *Miranda,* at point of arrest. However, it is quite clear that the right is present once an individual is taken into custody and interrogation begins. Thus one may be arrested and held without counsel during a reasonable period of time, but statements taken during such periods are not admissible in state and federal courts. An exception occurs if it can be shown that the defendant knowingly and intelligently waived his right to have retained or appointed counsel, but the Supreme Court has laid a heavy burden on the government to demonstrate that fact. Confessions, consequently, can still play some role in law enforcement, since any statement given freely and voluntarily without indication of compulsion is admissible. Such conditions are more likely to be established in a case in which a person comes to the police station or calls a police officer to offer a confession or other statements he may wish to make. A distinction is drawn when the individual is taken into custody or deprived of his freedom, and the burden of proving a voluntariness of verbal or written statements may be well-nigh insuperable. In any event, under the restrictions which the Court has imposed, it would seem much simpler, administratively, to see that defendant has counsel, employed or appointed, before any interrogation occurs.

Justices Byron White, John Marshall Harlan, and Potter Stewart dissented in *Miranda,* as did Justice Tom Clark. The first three justices, basically, rejected the view that interrogation in custody is inherently coercive. Apparently they would have preferred to continue with the earlier test, that is, whether the totality of circumstances constituted physical or psychological coercion to such a degree as to overbear the defendant's will at time of confession. Clark, on the other hand, saw the new rule as "a strict constitutional specific inserted at the nerve center of crime detection [that] may well kill the patient."[113] He also would have preferred to follow the totality of circumstances rule.

113 Ibid., p. 500.

Twelve

In comparing the right to counsel for military personnel tried by courts-martial with that of criminal defendants in civil courts, one is immediately struck with the disparity in the questions which appellate courts are frequently asked to decide. This is not totally unexpected, since the UCMJ specifically establishes certain trial rights which have been added to the federal Constitution through court decisions. The accused before a general or a special court-martial not only has the absolute right to be represented by civilian counsel if provided by him or by military counsel of his own selection if reasonably available, but Article 27 requires that defense counsel and assistant defense counsel be appointed. As a consequence, those attempting to overturn court-martial convictions have focused on the qualifications and behavior of counsel more frequently than have criminal defendants in civilian courts. A trial or defense counsel of a general court-martial must be a member of the judge advocate's corps. In addition, if he is not a graduate of an accredited law school, he must be a person who is a member of the bar of a federal court or of the highest court in a state. Moreover, whatever his other qualifications, trial and defense counsel of general courts must be certified as competent to perform such duties by the judge advocate general of the armed force of which he is a member.

Because of legally possible exceptions, the qualifications are somewhat less for counsel appointed to serve in special courts-martial. But the code requires that trial and defense counsel be similarly qualified. It has been held that the existence at the time a general court-martial is convened of appointed defense counsel qualified in the sense of Article 27 (b) is an indispensable prerequisite to the exercise of jurisdiction by the court.[114] The fact that qualified assistant defense counsel might have been appointed does not meet this requirement. If trial counsel before a special court-martial is certified as a member of a state bar, the defense counsel must be so certified. Otherwise, all proceedings will be null and void. In determining qualifications, however, military appellate bodies, as civilian appellate bodies, may not be swayed by irrelevancies. In *United States* v. *Davis*,[115] the defense counsel was a high school graduate with no professional education and little legal experience. Neither the assistant trial judge nor the assistant defense counsel was legally trained. The trial counsel, on the other hand, while not a member of the judge advocate general's corps nor of any bar, held a Bachelor's degree from the University of Pittsburgh and a law degree from Duquesne University. He had also enjoyed extensive legal experience in the army. Nevertheless, the Court of Military Appeals refused to reverse the conviction. Judge Paul W. Brosman, for the court, held that the record failed to disclose that legally trained counsel could have done more than the defense counsel. Consequently, the accused was not found to have been materially prejudiced by the disparity in qualification of counsel. The court has also held that while the appointment of a warrant officer as defense counsel constitutes error, inequality in rank does not necessarily establish prejudice. There is nothing in the code to require the appointment of an officer as counsel in a special court-martial. However, the *Manual of Courts Martial* (1951) does provide that both trial and defense counsel shall be officers. The language of the *Manual* has been interpreted as a clarification of the intent of the code.

114 *Butler* v. *United States* 8 C.M.R. 692.
115 2 C.M.R. 8, 1 U.S.C.M.A. 102.

Both the code and the USCMA are less lenient in regard to certain other qualifications. If trial counsel is qualified to act as counsel before a general court-martial, a defense counsel must be qualified similarly. And if the trial counsel is a judge advocate or a Military Judge or is licensed to practice in the federal courts or before the highest court of a state, the defense counsel must possess the same qualifications. In regard to these matters, the question is not whether the accused is represented by legally qualified counsel. A Board of Review has found fatal error and lack of jurisdiction in a situation in which trial counsel was a lawyer, appointed defense counsel was a nonlawyer who was excused with the consent of the accused and the accused was represented by individual counsel who was a lawyer within the terms of Article 27 (b) of the code.[116] As the board pointed out, the requirement is that appointed trial and defense counsel possess equivalent qualifications and that this requirement is distinct from the right of the accused to be represented by individual counsel.

The key case in this general area is *United States* v. *Edwin L. Culp,* decided in 1963.[117] Culp was tried and convicted by a special court-martial on six specifications of larceny. The proceedings were approved by the convening authority and the supervisory authority. Culp was a person of superior mental attainments and had an outstanding record in the Marine Corps. The order appointing the special court-martial designated two naval officers as trial counsel and two as defense counsel. None of the four were certified in accordance with Article 27. In reviewing the record on appeal, a Board of Review determined that the plea of guilty was improvident and that the record contained cumulative error. But more important, the board decided a constitutional question, that is, whether Culp was entitled under the Sixth Amendment to "counsel quali-

---

[116] *Cushing* v. *United States* 22 C.M.R. 673. Prior to Aug. 24, 1969, the Courts of Military Review were known as Boards of Review.
[117] 14 U.S.C.M.A. 199; Cf. *U.S.* v. *Cutting* 14 U.S.C.M.A. 347.

fied in the law unless such right was competently and intelligently waived by him."[118] The convictions and the sentence were set aside. The judge advocate general's office then certified the following questions to the USCMA: Was the board correct regarding rights under the Sixth Amendment? If so, in a trial by special court-martial, does military due process demand that "counsel qualified in the law" be qualified in the sense of Article 27 (b)?

In responding to these questions, the Court of Military Appeals was very quick to pronounce it totally unnecessary for the Board of Review to determine the constitutional question. Noting the reluctance of the Supreme Court to decide constitutional questions and the fact that the decision made by the board had the effect of denying to all constitutional courts, including the United States Supreme Court, any opportunity to review the question, the board was said to have acted hastily. Such a result flows from the provisions of the code governing review of board decisions by higher authority. Judge Paul J. Kilday suggested that numerous Boards of Review might reach different conclusions on such a far-reaching question, thereby creating considerable confusion. Under these circumstances, he thought it better for Boards to leave such matters to higher competent review authority.

Chief Justice Earl Warren has suggested that the USCMA is "a sort of civilian Supreme Court of the Military."[119] But members of the defense forces do not appear before courts-martial in a position identical to defendants before civilian courts. No serviceman appears before a court-martial alone and there are no indigents in the service. Other than paying his own individually retained counsel, the military defendant has all appropriate services rendered without any expense to him whatever. At the same time, the serviceman appearing before a court-martial is not governed solely by procedural rules necessary for civilian

118 Ibid., p. 201.
119 Earl Warren, "The Bill of Rights and the Military," p. 11.

defendants in criminal trials. The serviceman has the right to due process of law. He is protected against unreasonable search and seizure; he cannot be compelled to be a witness against himself. But, just as the United States Supreme Court has refused to hold that all provisions of the Bill of Rights apply to the states, the Court of Military Appeals has refused to hold that all such provisions apply to military trials. Both courts, in effect, have proceeded to examine each claim of deprivation of right as it has been presented. In so doing, different results have been reached. The military defendant has no right to trial by jury. And trial by court-martial is not required in "the State where the said crimes shall have been committed."[120]

By claiming that the code entitled him to a trained lawyer as counsel, Culp suggested that the meaning of "counsel" in the code was identical to the interpretation which the Supreme Court has given the word in the Sixth Amendment. Judge Paul J. Kilday was not convinced. Reading Article 27 in light of the law existing at the time of its enactment, and using analogous arguments from the Supreme Court's opinion in *Ex parte Quirin*,[121] he concluded that military officers were qualified as counsel prior to enactment of the code and that Article 27 made no change in the situation. Thus the finding that Culp was entitled to counsel under the Sixth Amendment was held in error. Chief Judge Robert E. Quinn agreed with the result reached but expressed the view that the Sixth Amendment right to counsel was indeed applicable to courts-martial. He found nothing in the Sixth Amendment, however, to prevent Congress from establishing qualifications for counsel and concluded that a lawyer was unnecessary under Article 27. Judge Homer Ferguson, concurring in the result, held that the Sixth Amendment applies to a court-martial but that Culp's counsel was entitled to practice at the bar of this court as other counsel are entitled to

120 United States Constitution, Art. III, Sec. 2.
121 317 U.S. 1.

practice at the bar of civilian courts. Consequently he saw no defect in the use of a nonlawyer. At the same time Ferguson expressed the view that it was unwise to use non-lawyer counsel in special courts-martial, and Quinn agreed with this position insofar as bad-conduct tribunals are concerned.

The position of Judge Quinn, and to some extent Judge Ferguson, has been shared by others. In the first session of the Eighty-ninth Congress a bill designed to upgrade the qualifications of military counsel in certain cases was introduced by Senator Sam J. Ervin, the chairman of the Senate Subcommittee on Constitutional Rights. This bill would prohibit a peacetime bad-conduct discharge unless the accused was represented at trial or given the opportunity to be represented by a defense counsel with qualifications not less than those prescribed under Article 27 (b) of the code. Since this provision describes the qualifications for trial or defense counsel appearing before a general court, the effect would be to impose upon special courts a higher level of qualification for counsel in bad-conduct discharge cases. In short, it would require "lawyer-counsel," which some have thought desirable. The evidence seems to indicate that a bad-conduct discharge has essentially the same effect as a dishonorable discharge, that is, one who receives such a discharge is stigmatized and restricted in various areas of endeavor. Such restrictions can be conceptualized as an encroachment upon life, liberty, or property or due process rights under the Fifth Amendment. In view of these considerations, it is argued that legally trained counsel is essential to the protection of due-process rights.

The bill also would require the right to similarly qualified counsel for servicemen who appear before nonjudicial discharge boards. These boards have the power to recommend an undesirable discharge. The counsel requirement would be limited, however, to peacetime on the ground that such procedures might be infeasible in wartime but, nevertheless, quite suitable otherwise. A number of interested organizations and individuals have supported these proposals including the American Civil Liberties Union, the American Veterans Committee, the American Legion, and the judges of the USCMA. Judge Quinn has recommended that the time-of-war exception be eliminated on the ground that the exercise of military power in time of war tends to be more arbitrary than in peacetime. Judge Ferguson also has supported this legislation very strongly pointing out that "the public does not distinguish between dishonorable and bad conduct discharges, nor between those awarded by a General Court-Martial or a Special Court-Martial. Indeed, except in a relatively unimportant area, the Veteran's Administration makes no such distinctions in withholding veteran's benefits. The non-lawyer Special Court Martial cases we have received, all of which, at the appellate level, involve bad conduct discharges, are frequently farcical. Where the penalty is so terrible and long-lasting, the accused should receive the benefit of legally qualified counsel."[122]

As a consequence of the interest of Senator Ervin and others, effective August 24, 1969, the Special Court is barred by the Military Justice Act from giving bad conduct discharges unless the accused is represented by lawyer-counsel.[123]

[122] U.S., Congress, Senate, *Joint Hearings on S750 before the Subcommittee on Constitutional Rights, Committee of Judiciary, and a Special Subcommittee of the Committee on Armed Services,* 89th Cong., 2d sess., 1966, p. 302.
[123] 82 Stat. 1336.

Thirteen

A second dimension that has attracted attention is that of counsel behavior during trial. Assuming that qualified counsel has been retained or appointed, a serviceman being tried by a court-martial has the right to competent and effective representation by counsel. Since it is a simple matter to charge counsel with inadequate representation, the Court of Military Appeals has consistently held that the competency of defense counsel cannot be impeached unless the complaining party is able to show disloyalty or gross carelessness which was of direct aid to the prosecution. This means, in effect, that errors in judgment alone are not sufficient to impeach the effectiveness or adequacy of counsel. The complaining party must show that representation by counsel was so inadequate that the proceedings bordered on the ridiculous or constituted an empty gesture.[124]

Defense counsel is required to carry out his obligations to the accused with vigor and dispatch and with imagination. He must take advantage of every procedural device available to him if there is a good possibility of strengthening his client's case thereby. It has been held that a military defendant was deprived of effective counsel where, in good faith, he asked his defense counsel to contest the voluntariness of a pretrial statement but was refused.[125] Counsel's argument that he refused to act upon the request because he foresaw little likelihood of success was rejected.

In a general court-martial which occurred in Germany, the appointed defense counsel did not consult prosecution witnesses prior to trial; there was no attempt to examine any member of the court on voir dire; and no preemptory challenge was exercised. Questions about court members' knowledge of the case, their views on the death sentence, and whether there had been discussion of the necessity of severe punishment were not asked even though the court was specially selected. During the trial only two objections were made and they concerned the involuntary character of certain confessions admitted as evidence. The defense counsel offered no objections to the instructions given; no testimony was offered on their merits; and no evidence was given to back the defendant's claim that his confessions were involuntary. Finally no attempt was made to avoid the death penalty ultimately meted out. The USCMA thought these facts were sufficient to show that there had been inadequate representation by defense counsel, and a new hearing was ordered.[126]

In other cases, the USCMA has expressly condemned situations in which defense counsel presents no evidence and makes no argument in mitigation in order to sustain an agreement with the convening authority regarding prior plea and the sentence to be pronounced. It is not illegal per se to "cop a plea," to make agreements prior to trial which may have the effect of reducing the charge and the sentence in certain cases. But where such agreements are made, the defense counsel must proceed at trial to present evidence in mitigation where such evidence is available, even at the risk of contravening the guilty plea. The position of the court on the importance of mitigating evidence is outlined clearly in *United States* v. *Broy*.[127] Broy was confined to a brig at the Marine Corps Air Station in El Toro, California, on charges of issuing bad checks. At trial, by general court-martial, defense counsel moved to dismiss the charges on the ground that more

124 *United States* v. *Huff* 11 U.S.C.M.A. 397.
125 *Oakley* v. *United States* 25 C.M.R. 624.
126 *United States* v. *Parker* 6 U.S.C.M.A. 75.
127 14 U.S.C.M.A. 419.

than three months had transpired between confinement and trial, thereby violating the accused's right to a speedy trial. He charged further that treatment accorded the accused in the brig constituted cruel and unusual punishment. Both motions were denied by the law officer. In the brig, Broy had been forced to rise at 4:30 A.M., given three minutes to dress, then engaged in physical exercise consisting of three hundred to four hundred step-ups, two hundred to two hundred and fifty pushups, and four to four and one-half hours of close order drill. This treatment aggravated Broy's knee trouble, caused him severe pain, and subjected him to the possibility of an operation to correct the condition. Being unable to walk to the mess hall, Broy was then compelled to eat cold food for two weeks. The failure of defense counsel to bring all these facts to the attention of the court in possible mitigation of court findings and sentence was held to be reversible error.

Sometimes the counsel behavior complained of is not in the class of omissions but involves overt action taken by defense counsel which adversely affects the rights of his client. In one instance, an enlisted man in the air force who became a member of the Jehovah's Witnesses sect was ordered to report to his place of duty and refused. He was then sent to see his commanding officer, whom he refused to salute. When ordered to his place of duty by the commanding officer he did not go.

Before a general court he was convicted and sentenced for failure to salute and failure to report to a place of duty as ordered. Subsequent to conviction the appointed defense counsel stated that "The defense counsel feels very strongly that the accused has committed some serious offenses against the United States Air Force and should be justly and properly punished therefor."[128] It is unlikely that a statement of this kind would be made by legal counsel in a civilian court. Were this to occur, it is a foregone conclusion that an appellate body would remand for

128 *Cupp* v. *United States* 24 C.M.R. 573.

consideration of sentence or possibly reverse the sentence on the grounds that assigned defense counsel with such emotional commitments could not have adequately discharged his obligations to his client. In the instant case, however, a Board of Review held that while it was error for the defense counsel to predicate such a statement on the basis of strong personal feelings, the impropriety constituted no more than an error of judgment which did not render otherwise adequate representation inadequate. Nevertheless, the board reduced the sentence or the hard labor portion of the sentence to nine months.

The USCMA has been a little more severe with counsel behavior of this type. In *United States* v. *McFarlane*,[129] the accused was charged with the murder of one victim and assault with intent to murder a second. At trial, the defense counsel allowed his client to plead guilty to a charge of assault with intent to murder. A plea of not guilty was made to the murder charge, but the defense counsel then stated that he wished to inform the court that the code precluded a plea of guilty to the murder charge. Subsequently, during trial, he permitted the prosecution to present its case with little hindrance or interference; he made no attempt to develop an issue as to his client's mental capacity to entertain a specific intent, although the pretrial investigating officer had specifically recommended a psychiatric examination; and finally, defense counsel waived argument at the conclusion of the case.

The Court of Military Appeals found such tactics to require a reversal and a rehearing. Here the court found at least a violation of the spirit of the code and this, coupled with counsel's other behavior, constituted inadequate representation.

In *United States* v. *Winchester*[130] a soldier was charged with larceny of rifles for sale in Tijuana, Mexico. He pleaded guilty at a general court-martial and retained individual military counsel. During the trial Winchester

129 8 U.S.C.M.A. 96.
130 12 U.S.C.M.A. 74.

asked to testify and was permitted to do so. At the close of his statement, however, his counsel asked to be relieved of the role of counsel on the grounds that Winchester had committed perjury. The USCMA held that the concept of adequate representation precluded such behavior on the part of counsel and a rehearing on the sentence was ordered.

Fourteen

In exercising his right to individual counsel, the military defendant may choose a civilian lawyer or a military person. The qualifications required for appointed defense counsel are not imposed on individual counsel. If the defendant chooses a military officer as individual counsel, that officer is not required to be qualified in the sense of Article 27 (b). However, the serviceman making such a choice must run the risk of any damage accruing from inadequate representation. One who is convicted in a general court may not complain that he was inadequately represented by his own deliberately selected counsel. In *Adams* v. *Hiatt*,[131] the accused personally selected a major and a captain to represent him in a general court-martial on a charge of rape. Subsequently the court excused the regularly appointed defense counsel. Subsequent to conviction, Adams claimed that the officers chosen did not adequately represent him. A Pennsylvania district court held that such a claim was untenable where free choice as to individual counsel had been exercised.

An early case decided by the USCMA on this point is *United States* v. *Hunter*.[132] Hunter was charged with murdering two Koreans and raping a ten-year-old Korean girl in April 1951, was convicted on all three charges, and sentenced to death. At trial, Hunter was represented by two officers one of whom was a member of the Quartermaster Corps who was not qualified under Article 27 (b) of the code. Nevertheless, he was selected by Hunter as his personal representative. The other officer was appointed by the convening authority and was a captain in the Judge Advocate General's Corps who had the necessary qualifications and who had appeared in many trials. During trial, both counsel were present, accessible, presented arguments, made cross-examinations, and both disclosed good knowledge of the working rules of evidence. Hearsay evidence and conclusions were objected to, appropriate motions were made, and a theory of defense—lack of identification—was developed. The Court of Military Appeals thought military due process was fully met here. Recognizing that it may be desirable to furnish every accused with a mature and experienced trial lawyer, the court said that such was an impossibility. The best that can be done is to assure the appointment of officers who are reasonably well qualified to protect the substantial rights of the accused.

While the qualifications *required* of defense counsel appearing before special courts-martial are less than those for counsel appearing before general courts, a convening authority cannot legally appoint an enlisted man to serve as defense counsel. The code itself does not bar such appointment but it does not authorize it and the appointment of such counsel has been held to constitute error. This was the holding in *United States* v. *Long*,[133] a case in which both the defense counsel and trial counsel were not lawyers in the sense of Article 27. The trial counsel was a first lieutenant in the Marine Corps while the defense counsel was an aviation chief machinist mate in the navy. The judge advocate on the staff of the officer exercising general court-martial jurisdiction argued that, even so, there was no prejudice to the accused and that the conviction should stand. In reversing the judgment, Judge Latimer rejected this argument saying, "It is obvious that when an accused pleads guilty, it is impossible to appraise fairly defense counsel's worth. However, as a general proposition, and

131 79 F. Supp. 433.
132 2 U.S.C.M.A. 37.
133 5 U.S.C.M.A. 572.

when dealing with non-lawyers, the judgment, knowledge of military law, experience, and training of officers ought to teach them to be wiser and more judicious legal advisors than enlisted men."[134]

From this brief survey, it is quite evident that the USCMA (and Boards of Review in some instances) have dealt primarily with limited types of "right to counsel" questions. These may be summarized as follows: (1) What special meanings are to be attached to the qualifications required of appointed defense counsel and individual counsel appearing before general and special courts-martial? (2) What relative sets of qualifications for trial and defense counsel satisfy the equivalency requirement? (3) What are permissible, impermissible, and required behaviors of appointed defense counsel in general and special courts-martial?

Since all defendants before general and special courts are guaranteed counsel by the UCMJ, the military system has been free of the *Gideon* question, that is, who has a right to have counsel appointed in state courts. The code answers: in the military system, all criminal defendants appearing before general and special courts possess such a right. At the same time, the Supreme Court has not been plagued with cases concerning counsel's qualifications and behavior at trial.[135] Since counsel in civilian courts must be admitted to the bar of the court before which they practice, adequate qualifications are assumed once admission has been gained. In this regard, the requirements of the code are more restrictive and perhaps operate to assure with a greater degree of certainty that the right of the criminal defendant will be scrupulously protected. This is not to say that the right to counsel before military courts is more valuable or broader in scope than the privilege in civilian courts. This appears to be the case before general courts-martial

[134] Ibid., p. 200.
[135] Federal lower courts have occasionally reversed for improper counsel behavior. *Johnson* v. *United States* 110 F. 2d. 562.

but not before special courts. Nevertheless, whatever the scope of the right, that which is given is more meaningful where appellate bodies view closely the behavior of counsel at trial and where the required qualifications of counsel are of a higher order. While William M. Beaney reports that military defendants had little luck with claims of ineffectual counsel in an earlier period,[136] recent decisions by the Court of Military Appeals have insisted on high standards of behavior for appointed counsel.

The question of equivalently qualified counsel for prosecution and defense is not, of course, an issue in civilian courts. The use of the "public defender," perhaps, touches this conceptual area. But it is safe to say in the civilian system that money buys talent and that appointed counsel are unlikely to be of the same "rank" as the prosecutor. At the same time, the superiority of the civilian system in requiring legally qualified or lawyer-counsel in all criminal trials is reflected in proposals to extend lawyer-counsel rights to special courts-martial. While the military defendant has no right to counsel before the one-officer summary court-martial, the code does not require that he be tried by such a court. He can, in any case, implement his right to be tried by a general or special court. As a consequence, the right to counsel at the summary level is of lesser importance. A continuation of current trends, however, may eventually lead to the establishment of counsel rights at the summary court stage, or the elimination of the summary court itself.

[136] Beaney, *The Right to Counsel in American Courts,* p. 53.

Fifteen

Having said all this is in no way to suggest that the USCMA and the Supreme Court have found no common problems in the right to counsel area in recent years. Indeed, both courts have had to face the question "At what stage of criminal proceedings is counsel necessary?" The Supreme Court has required counsel at the critical stage, at the point at which the arrested person has become the focal object of a particular investigation and whenever, after arrest, interrogation begins. The Court of Military Appeals reached similar conclusions somewhat earlier than the Supreme Court.

Under Article 32 the person accused of violating military law who is to be tried before a general court possesses certain rights to counsel at the investigatory stage. He may be represented by civilian counsel, if provided by him, or by military counsel of his own selection if such is reasonably available, or by counsel appointed by the officer exercising general court-martial jurisdiction over the command. Appointed defense counsel at the investigatory stage must meet all the qualifications of Article 27 (b). But the court has held that where the counsel appointed was not certified under 27 (b) and no objection was made, and no objection of prejudice of the accused's rights was offered at trial, and where the representation provided appears to have been adequate, there is no violation of the code.[137] While a plea of guilty waives all defects that are neither jurisdictional nor a deprivation of due process of law, waiver may also be accomplished in other ways. If there is a denial of right to counsel at the investigatory stage but no objection is made at trial, the Court of Military Appeals will assume a waiver of the privilege.

Sometimes the question of counsel may arise in a situation unique to the military system. For example, in *United States* v. *Nichols*,[138] the accused was a counterintelligence agent. At the initial investigation, certain information was collected, marked confidential, and classified. The defendant obtained civilian counsel and requested his presence at the investigatory hearing. This request was denied on the grounds that the civilian counsel selected by the accused had not been cleared for classified material. The convening authority was then requested to initiate security clearance for the civilian counsel, but this request was denied without comment. Although civilian counsel then initiated and obtained clearance for himself, such clearance was not forthcoming until after the investigation had been completed. Consequently, the accused was represented at the hearing by his appointed counsel only.

The court found this series of events to violate Nichols's rights under the code. The accused military person has the right to be represented by civilian counsel instead of appointed military counsel. If civilian counsel can be barred from a court-martial as a security risk, the court held that the burden is on the government to initiate and complete those procedures leading to such a classification. Short of that, it is error to exclude a civilian counsel from a pretrial investigation as a security risk.

Does the serviceman have the right to consult with his attorney upon being taken into custody? The USCMA provided some answers to this question in *United States* v. *Brown*[139] and *United States* v. *Gunnels*.[140]

Gunnels was the commanding officer at Amarillo Air

137 *United States* v. *Steveson* 9 U.S.C.M.A. 332.
138 8 U.S.C.M.A. 119.
139 13 U.S.C.M.A. 14.
140 8 U.S.C.M.A. 130.

Force Base in Texas. During his off-duty hours, Airman Hill was employed in a civilian capacity. Consequently, he often fell asleep in his classes and on other occasions failed to report for duty. After a number of difficulties, Gunnels offered Hill an honorable discharge for two to three hundred dollars. On a pretext, Hill was given emergency leave and traveled to his home to raise the money. He subsequently wired two hundred dollars to Gunnels and then awaited his *quid pro quo*. Shortly after the transmission of the money, however, Gunnels was transferred and made secretary of the officers' mess. Consequently, the plan to obtain the discharge was aborted and Hill was transferred to an air base in Idaho. His money was not refunded. Two months later, Gunnels was charged with making false official statements in connection with his duties. After a general court-martial was scheduled, Gunnels wrote Hill asking him to furnish affidavits containing false statements and Hill complied. Using Hill's statement, Gunnels's lawyer was able to get the charges dropped. But in the interim, he sent Hill a list of questions and suggested answers. Hill took the questions to his commanding officer and reported his dealings with Gunnels. When confronted with this evidence, Gunnels stated that he wished to make no statement until he had an opportunity to consult with counsel. He was then permitted to go to the office of the staff judge advocate with instructions that he return immediately. But the staff judge advocate was informed of the pending visit and ordered all legal officers in his office not to assist Gunnels. He emphasized that if the front office got wind of any assistance, heads would roll. When Gunnels arrived, he was told that no assistance could be furnished. He then returned and answered questions put to him by agents of the government including a denial that he received money from Hill. This denial was later charged as a false official statement on interrogation.

At trial, Gunnels moved to dismiss on the ground that he was denied military due process by being denied counsel at interrogation. The USCMA agreed with this contention citing *Powell* v. *Alabama* and other cases. The court pointed out that a criminal proceeding must be distinguished from investigations by law enforcement officers. In the criminal proceeding the right to assigned counsel exists. But the military person has not been entitled to appointed counsel prior to the filing of charges against him. Nevertheless, the court stressed that the distinction between criminal proceedings and investigations does not mean that a person suspected of crime can be prohibited from *consulting* counsel. The right to obtain necessary legal advice at the investigatory stage cannot be diminished. The staff judge advocate was obligated to give Gunnels correct advice and had he done so, the court suggested, the accused would have known he had a right to consult his own counsel during interrogation.

In *Brown,* the court again held that if the accused seeks to exercise his right to consult with counsel during interrogation, he must be afforded an opportunity to do so.

While *Gunnels* established the *Escobedo* right prior to *Escobedo* and *Brown* reaffirmed that right, neither case offered the privileges extended by the Supreme Court in the *Miranda* case. This omission did not flow from the failure to raise the question. In 1966 the USCMA was called upon to decide whether the right to counsel in military law extended to the investigative processes. The court answered, "Nothing in the Uniform Code . . . or in the decisions of this Court, and nothing in our experience with military methods of interrogation, indicate that the only feasible way to give maximum protection to the Constitutional right to the assistance of counsel is that the accused have counsel beside him during police questioning."[141] Thus, it found an incriminating statement given by the accused in a police interrogation admissible as evidence even though the accused had no counsel during questioning

[141] *United States* v. *Wimberley*, 16 U.S.C.M.A. 3, 10.

and was not advised of his right to consult with counsel during interrogation.

Four months later the Supreme Court decided *Miranda* v. *Arizona*. At least one of the services revealed a sensitivity to this decision of the civilian high court. Upon learning of it, the air force immediately directed all air police to comply with the mandate of *Miranda* until military courts could decide the direction to be taken, if any, in military law. The opportunity to decide the issue was presented in *United States* v. *Tempia*.[142] Mike Tempia was convicted by general court-martial of taking indecent liberties with females under the age of sixteen. After being advised that he had the right to retain civilian counsel at his own expense and that he would not have the right to appointed counsel until charges were preferred or a pretrial investigation convened, Tempia confessed.

The arguments before the Court of Military Appeals revolved around the *Miranda* holding and are of some interest in themselves. Tempia's trial commenced one day after *Miranda* took effect. At the court-martial, his counsel, on the basis of news reports of *Miranda,* sought to have Tempia's confession excluded. He was not successful. On appeal, the United States was represented by the air force, since this was an air force court-martial. The judge advocate general of the navy, however, filed an *amicus curiae* brief. The government as party to the case and the government as navy took two different approaches. First, it was argued that while the Constitution protects the serviceman's right to counsel, *Miranda* dealt only with procedural devices designed to enforce a constitutional right in the exercise of the Supreme Court's supervisory powers. Therefore, the military court was not required to follow *Miranda* and indeed, the argument went, it would be unwise to adopt such procedures in the military system. The judge advocate general (navy), on the other hand, took the position that

142 16 U.S.C.M.A. 629; cf. *United States* v. *Hardy,* 17 U.S.C.M.A. 100.

constitutional limitations do not affect military law and therefore the principles of *Miranda* were inapplicable. This position is best interpreted as strategical. The USCMA has noted the applicability of the Constitution on a number of occasions and has specifically held that the right to non-lawyer counsel is guaranteed to accused servicemen by the Sixth Amendment.

The advantages inherent in having representatives of the government present two positions, either of which if adopted would result in affirmance of Tempia's conviction are obvious. The procedure permits the pressing of two incompatible arguments which would be somewhat difficult if the government's position were limited to that put forth by appointed counsel only. In any event, the court, citing earlier cases, held that constitutional safeguards apply to military trials except insofar as they are made inapplicable either expressly or by necessary implication.

In response to the second argument, the court concluded that *Miranda* laid down constitutional rules and not merely rules of procedure under its supervisory powers. This position was more difficult to reach on the basis of the language used in *Miranda*. However, finding support in a later case,[143] Judge Homer Ferguson's opinion held that *Miranda* "lays down concrete rules which are to govern all criminal interrogations by Federal or State authorities, military or civilian, if resulting statements are to be used in trials commencing on and after June 13, 1966."[144]

Since *Miranda* dealt with custodial interrogation, it was necessary to identify the stage of military proceedings which, by analogy, may constitute a similar situation. Here the court declined to require technical custody, pointing out that in the military system a suspect may be required to report for questioning without the necessities of warrants or other legal processes. Consequently, the test adopted was one which would cover such eventuality, that is,

[143] *Johnson* v. *New Jersey*, 384 U.S. 719.
[144] *Tempia*, p. 635.

whether the suspect has been deprived of his freedom of action in any significant way. While the military suspect may waive counsel, the USCMA has adopted the skeptical posture of the Supreme Court which places the burden of proving waiver on the government.

Finally, the government argued, unsuccessfully, that counsel could not be appointed during the interrogation of Tempia, since no funds for that purpose had been appropriated. This was an ingenious argument, since Congress could not have specifically appropriated funds to provide counsel for Tempia at interrogation prior to the establishment of the right itself. But sidestepping this technicality, Judge Ferguson pointed out that Congress has provided funds for defense counsel and that there is nothing in the UCMJ or the *Manual of Courts Martial* to prevent the use of such funds for counsel at interrogation.

The *Tempia* case produced a concurring opinion by Judge Paul J. Kilday and a dissenting opinion by Chief Judge Robert E. Quinn. While agreeing with Ferguson, Kilday added some thoughts of his own which may portend certain trends for the future. Historical review led him to conclude that the USCMA is bound on constitutional questions by the Supreme Court and that the actions of the USCMA are subject to review in the civil courts. The former point was certainly not clear at the adoption of the UCMJ and was controverted in early cases. As in the stance taken by the judge advocate general (navy), the matter is not yet clear to all eyes. The latter conclusion seems contrary to the traditional view that review in the civil courts is limited to questions of jurisdiction and also undermines the language in the code on the finality of court-martial judgments after military review.

Chief Judge Quinn saw *Miranda* in a different light. For him, the key was whether the Supreme Court intended its ruling to apply to the military system. This question he answered in the negative. The Supreme Court, he said, merely attempted to establish procedures for safeguarding certain rights, such procedures being not the only permissible ones but procedures which would suffice given the practices in the Arizona jurisdiction. The question for Quinn, then, was whether, given the practices in the military system, the military safeguards were sufficient to protect the right of the accused. This he affirmed.

Quinn's position cannot be brushed aside as easily as the majority judges might have liked. If one takes the *Miranda* and *Escobedo* rulings and compares them with military practice, the results are somewhat striking. In the first place, the *Escobedo* rule that right to consult counsel exists at the custodial interrogation stage was adopted by the USCMA in *Gunnels*.

While this right covered civilian counsel if the accused could afford it, it also included the right to be advised during interrogation by a member of the staff judge advocate's office. Included among the rights of which the accused might be advised are the requirements of Article 31 of the UCMJ. Under that article, the suspect must be specifically informed of the nature of the accusation against him, of his right to remain silent, and that anything he says may be used against him. Since *Miranda* established the right to similar warnings on the civil side, the serviceman had greater protection than the civilian for a period of fifteen years. In fact, in deciding *Miranda,* the Supreme Court remarked on this discrepancy saying that the civilian ought to have at least as much protection of the right to remain silent as the military suspect. Thus, it cannot be said that the military system is indebted to the Supreme Court for recognizing the value of that particular safeguard.

We are now brought to the question of appointed counsel during interrogation and the necessity of advising a suspect that he has such a right. Here, military law and the law of *Miranda* did indeed differ. Traditionally, appointed counsel has not been available in the military system prior to the drawing of charges. Whether this difference requires a change in military practice, even assuming that the

Supreme Court makes law for the military, depends on whether *Miranda* is read literally. If the goal is to protect the individual from having his will overborne by having counsel advise him that he has the right to remain silent and that what he says may be used against him, then the staff judge advocate can do this as well as a civilian attorney or the serviceman's appointed military counsel. However, a further consideration is evident. While the staff judge advocate, prior to *Miranda,* was available for consultation and required to advise a suspect of his rights, there is nothing in early cases or military law to obligate the staff judge advocate's office to advise an accused further if he decides to allow interrogation. Decisions as to what questions to answer, how to answer them, when to shut off interrogation, or certain areas of questioning—these and other matters would seem to require the kind of consultation that is only likely to result from the client-counsel relationship which exists between appointed or employed counsel. Consequently, there is no question that to apply *Miranda* to military law is to enhance the protections previously provided the serviceman who finds his freedom significantly reduced by military authority. This application has now been made through the decision in *Tempia.*

It may be said then that the Supreme Court has required appointed counsel at the stage that counsel becomes critical for protecting a suspect's right to a fair trial. The USCMA, traditionally, has operated under the same general rule. While the Supreme Court formulated and adopted its own rule, the principle was imposed on the USCMA by the Uniform Code of Military Justice. The Supreme Court has been involved in pushing back the point at which criminal process is critical for a suspect finally reaching the stage of "custodial interrogation" in *Miranda.* The USCMA, on the other hand, has been required from the outset to enforce the appointment of counsel at the point at which charges are drawn or a preliminary hearing is convened, but not before. This requirement is clearly stated in Article 32 of the code.[145] But the extension of the *Miranda* rights to the military suspect not only illustrates that constitutional law can grow in the USCMA as in the Supreme Court, it shows that the USCMA is not necessarily deterred in contributing to such growth by the exigencies of the military system.

Finally, it may be noted that legally qualified counsel is required in general courts but not in special and summary courts-martial. Yet, *Tempia* requires that servicemen be provided counsel at interrogation. This suggests the possibility that those who, subsequent to interrogation, are tried by the two lesser courts would have counsel provided in pretrial proceedings but not at trial. Such an anomaly would certainly increase the pressure from lay and professional critics to broaden the right of the military defendant to appointed, legally qualified counsel in all cases tried by courts-martial.

[145] For General Court prisoners only.

Sixteen

In summarizing, we have interpreted the concern of the public with the rights and obligations of the *Pueblo* crewmen in 1968 and 1969 as reflecting, in part, a broader, long-term interest in military justice. The behavioral controls imposed on the American serviceman and those who prosecute him, coupled with the institutional structure in which such prosecution occurs, have attracted the steady attention of particular publics during most of this century. This study suggests that these publics have been effective in promoting reform.

Our expectation that the liberalization of military law through acts of Congress would correlate with the use of large numbers of citizen draftees is borne out by the evidence. On the assumption that per capita abuse and deprivation rates have been constant, increase in numbers alone could account for the increased pressures which resulted in ameliorative action by the American Congress. But we have also suggested that the draftee is more likely to aspire to the principles and procedures of the larger society and its legal system than the professional military man who may subjugate such values to military expediency. In addition, it may be surmised that a citizenry through time becomes more enlightened and makes demands in a later period that would not occur earlier. The legal profession must also be credited with a hand in whatever improvements have been made, since lawyers who served or participated in the military legal system have often been at the forefront of those pushing for change. This leadership should not be underestimated in accounting for the revisions that have occurred.

In comparing "progress" on the military side with developments regarding right to counsel on the civilian side, we may find ourselves unhappy with both legal systems. Although federal courts, and to some extent state courts, have provided more substantial rights in the counsel area than military courts, little improvement was made on either side for the first hundred years. When improvements did begin to occur, they took place in the military system first, that is, in 1916 when the military defendant was specifically accorded the right to counsel of his own selection if reasonably available and in 1920 when he gained the right to appointed counsel before general and special courts. In 1920 it can be said that the military right was superior, insofar as a guarantee is concerned, to the same privilege in state and federal courts. At least such is true as regards assistance at trial. At the same time, the right to counsel in federal capital cases meant the right to lawyer-counsel whereas the military counsel was not required to be so qualified. Lawyer-counsel was not required in military courts until 1948 and then only if reasonably available. On the other hand, if trial counsel was qualified as an attorney, defense counsel was required to be similarly qualified. What we observe, then, is a two-dimensional difference between the right to counsel in military and civilian courts. One concerns the question of who has the right to appointed counsel and the other the qualifications of the counsel required to be appointed.

The civilian system has led and continues to lead the military system on the second dimension, since the Supreme Court has interpreted counsel in the Sixth Amendment to mean lawyer-counsel. New legislation in 1950 established the right of the military defendant to lawyer-counsel, but only in general courts. Thus, at present, the military defendant may stand before a special court-martial without lawyer-counsel. On the other dimension, the military system was somewhat ahead of its civilian counterpart from 1920 to 1938. By its decision in *Johnson* v. *Zerbst,* the Supreme Court required appointed counsel for indigent defendants in all federal criminal prosecutions. Since lawyer-counsel was required, one may say that since 1938, the right to counsel in federal courts has been superior to the right before courts-martial.

In comparing the military right with that granted in state courts, the military right to appointed nonlawyer counsel existed before any national or federal standard was imposed on the states. In 1932 the Supreme Court began to liberalize or enlarge the right to appointed counsel in state courts, and this has been carried through to conclusion in *Gideon, Escobedo,* and *Miranda.* Thus, at present, both state and military courts require appointed counsel in criminal trials. But the states, like the federal courts, are only required to furnish counsel to indigents. The military system, since 1948, has required the appointment of defense counsel without regard to the accused's ability to provide for his own counsel. Theoretically, this could improve the probability that a military defendant would have adequate representation. For one's financial resources could be such as to enable provision of counsel while not permitting the employment of "superior" legal talent.

With the 1950 legislation, the military system has finally incorporated the right to lawyer-counsel in important cases. But even with this "advanced legislation," counsel are not required to be appointed for summary courts, and nonlawyer counsel, under appropriate circumstances, may be appointed in special courts. Of course, we should not overlook the time consumed by the thousands of summary courts held each year. A military commander with 2,000 men in his charge may have to conduct twelve to twenty-five summary courts before breakfast each morning. Were all such cases surrounded with a panoply of exacting legal rules which some reformers suggest, it would be impossible for the commander to continue to preside. A proper perspective on the question is gained, perhaps, by comparing the summary court with the police court or traffic court on the civilian side. Both try massive numbers of minor offenses. In neither has it been historically necessary to provide the procedural rights which operate as a matter of course where more serious offenses are charged. In any event, the ability of the accused to avoid the summary court altogether operates to make the question of appointed counsel somewhat academic, though some would surely challenge this evaluation.

A possible problem area remains the discrepancy between the requirement of lawyer-counsel in civilian courts and the possible use of nonlawyer counsel in special courts-martial. One may venture the prediction that this discrepancy will be eliminated in the not-distant future. It will disappear as a result of the same pressures that have produced other changes, that is, the facts that a more protective procedure exists in the civilian system and that large numbers of draftees know and appreciate the civilian right.

The military system, in other respects, incorporates protections that might be beneficial in state and federal courts. The requirement of equivalent competence and training for trial and defense counsel before special courts is one such provision, since prosecutors and appointed defense attorneys in civilian courts are frequently ill matched.

In considering the decisions of Boards of Review and the United States Court of Military Appeals in the period 1951-1967, and comparing these decisions with those of the Supreme Court touching the right to counsel, we have noted the greater emphasis of the military system on the behavior of counsel after appointment. Appointed defense counsel must conduct himself at trial in a responsible manner and must exhibit in his behavior a serious intention to present his client's case in the best possible light. Relevant here are not only the routine responsibilities of the defense counsel. Opportunities for improving his case and mitigating the severity of judgment and sentence must be exploited. Since failure to exercise due effort may result in reversal, grounds for reversal are, in effect, in the defense counsel's hands. Appellate bodies have said that actual prejudice to the defendant must be shown to justify reversal. The USCMA has found sufficient prejudice in a single misstatement by defense counsel. But such determinations are, by necessity, subjective and must be made on an *ad hoc* basis. As a consequence, it should not be surprising to find that the Supreme Court has been relatively unwilling to entertain similar issues.

To observe a dissimilarity in some of the issues being decided by military and civilian courts is not to suggest that similar issues are not being faced and decided in other areas. The Court of Military Appeals has encountered and decided some of the same questions faced by the Supreme Court in recent years. For some years, both civilian and military defendants have been entitled to appointed counsel at time of charging. But the USCMA has held that the Sixth Amendment right to lawyer-counsel does not apply to accused military persons. That court has also lagged behind the Supreme Court in determining the stage of criminal process at which counsel must be appointed. However, the interpretation given counsel before general courts is equivalent to if not more encompassing than the Sixth Amendment counsel required by the Supreme Court. And the opinion of the USCMA in *Tempia* would put law enforcement agents at a greater disadvantage than civil police agents operating under the restrictions of *Miranda*. While it is true that *Tempia* was a general court case, it is possible that the restrictions enunciated will be applicable equally to special court cases or, to press the logic, summary court cases. This, unquestionably, would encourage greater care in summoning criminal suspects and promote greater attention to the accumulation of evidence prior to such summoning.

In the final analysis, then, the comparative practical status of counsel rights in military and civilian court systems are fairly equivalent regarding the point at which consultative rights and provided assistance attach. Rather than the point of assistance, the major disparity remains the possible use of nonlawyer counsel at certain stages in the military system and the impossibility of such occurrences in the civilian system.

Finally, one may comment on the steady drawing together of the practices and procedures governing military and civilian courts in American criminal trials over the past forty years. This has occurred during a period in which civilian rights have been enlarged and is a commentary on the American political system with its effective channels of communication to relevant policymakers. Without this structure, the changes we have observed would be very unlikely as attested by the fact that our experience in this area is not matched elsewhere.

Index